D1237801

Inventory
Record Accuracy

Inventory Record Accuracy

Unleashing the Power of Cycle Counting

Roger B. Brooks
Larry W. Wilson

John Wiley & Sons, Inc.

New York • Chichester • Brisbane • Toronto • Singapore

Dedication

To the women of my life, you wonderful people who have made me old, fat, and grey before my time. May you always remain as fastidious and intriguing in life, as you are in my memory. Linda, Louise, Barbara, Robin, and HeeBee GeeBee, I love you all.

RBB
Portland, Oregon

This book is dedicated to my family. First and foremost, to my wife of 25 years, Beverly. Without her loving support, honest critiques, and sometimes not so gentle nudges, this book would not have become a reality. I am convinced it is her advice and counsel that are at the root of my success. Second, to my children, Travis, Erin, and Ian. They have provided me tremendous joy and numerous opportunities for personal growth. To my daughter-in-law, Kristi, who has been an added blessing to my family. And last, but not least, to my grandson, Taylor John Wilson. For he, at the moment, represents the future of my family.

LWW
West Linn, Oregon

Acknowledgments

While the authors receive much of the credit, writing a book is very much a team effort. This book is no exception in that regard, and we would like to acknowledge the following people:

First, we would like to thank our publisher, Jim Childs, for keeping us on schedule, and making this book a reality. He reflected tremendous patience with our many changes. To Richard A. Luecke for integrating many thoughts, ideas, and technical concepts into a readable text. He truly made a "value added" contribution.

Next, we would like to thank all the people who took their time to review the book, and give us their honest critique and opinions.

From The Oliver Wight Companies: Patrick Bettini, Jim Correll, Walter Goddard, Darryl Landvater, and Christopher Turner.

From industry: Don Blem and Mal Irvine of Advanced Technology Labs, Robert Henderson of Aero-Design Technologies, Brandon Bidwell of Amoco Production, Adam Szczepanski of Baxter Diagnostics, John and Betty MacGregor of BMY, Russ Steele of Diamond Cabinets, Ron Stull of Evergreen Aviation, W. Dale Lockart of Fred Meyer, Ed Campbell and Bob Miller of Keystone Steel & Wire Company, Rick Burris, Mickey Clemens, and John Dietz, all of Martin Marietta Corporation, Robert Ouimet and Nicola Pellicciotti of Pratt & Whitney Canada, Phil Ruffner of Sunstrand Fluid Handling, and Grace Pastiak of Tellabs.

Others: Linda Brooks, Wade Brooks of Brooks & Associates, Professor Ed Davis of the University of Virginia, Paul Moore of Ernst &

Young, Professor Jerry Murphy of Portland State University, William Sandras, Dana Scannell, Ron Schultz, and Beverly Wilson.

And to those who did whatever needed to be done to get the art work and manuscripts distributed; Larada Johnson, Debbie Peck, and Traci Sheraden.

We sincerely thank each and every one of you for your contributions.

Roger and Larry

Contents

x   *Contents*

Introduction

Someone had to write this book. Inventory remains an important part of our manufacturing, distribution, and retail infrastructure. And no one wants to talk or write about it. Managing this critical resource starts with creating and maintaining accurate inventory records. But inventory and inventory record accuracy are not subjects that demand profound reflection in our business schools. However, when this investment goes afoul, it is often the subject of board meetings, executive council, financial crisis, and marketing strategy meetings. It seems inventory and inventory record accuracy only become important when they aren't working properly, much like our critical body functions.

Too many times, the authors have visited companies that didn't understand the purpose of inventory or how to track it. It was simply something "out there" in manufacturing, distribution, and in the stores that was a necessary evil. But the fact remains that manufacturing must have inventory. Distribution must have inventory. And retailing must have inventory. The notion of "Zero Inventory" will never be achieved as long as products are made, distributed, and sold. Even in the best cases of Just-in-Time manufacturing some inventory exists in the manufacturing conversion process. And it must be tracked in some way or another. Thus, inventory in manufacturing, distribution, and retailing is as necessary an evil as money. That is, you must have it to do business. More isn't always better; nor is less always better. However, knowing how much you have and need to operate your business is *always* better.

Knowing what you have, is what this book is all about. It is as basic to business as marketing, sales, manufacturing, purchasing, and accounting. Doing it right is a joy. Doing it wrong is unacceptable.

Roger B. Brooks
Sunriver, Oregon
October 1992

Inventory
Record Accuracy

Chapter One

The Company Bank

Where did it go? You open your wallet and discover that the $100 you withdrew from the bank just two days earlier is now a mere $3—not enough walking-around money for the rest of the day. A quick glance at the checkbook register indicates that there are still a few hundred dollars in your account, so at lunchtime you rush to the bank, write another check for $100, and enter the amount in the check register. The bank teller takes your check and keys your account number into his terminal. Yes, your balance will accommodate the amount of the check. Carefully, the teller counts the cash. When you ask for your computerized balance, the teller writes it down. Miraculously, the figure before you matches the balance in your register. With the cash tucked into your wallet, and the balance of your assets safely stored in the bank, you are once again ready to get on with your business.

Both you and your bank have been scrupulous in maintaining an accurate accounting of your personal assets. Why would we want to treat the inventory of our companies any differently? Shouldn't the records we keep for that inventory be as accurate and complete as those kept for our own bank accounts? For most companies, inventory is their greatest short-term asset. Yet few treat it that way. A careful examination of inventories for American manufacturing companies would find more than half of them inaccurate. In some companies, this is a real paradox. A company carrying $15 million in inventory may easily be off in its accounting by half a million. The same company will proudly boast that its $500 petty cash account is accurate to the penny. For some mysterious reason, business executives track currency closely, but as soon as that currency is converted into material, parts, or products, their interest or ability to account for them breaks down.

If a company's inventory records are inaccurate, that company cannot really know the state of its inventory assets. And without that knowledge, its ability to schedule or deliver what its customers want is significantly impaired. That impairment translates into a number of different costs, each of which reduces profits and hamstrings operations. Individuals who do not maintain accurate checking records pay for their negligence in the form of maintaining excess cash balances (to guard against overdrafts), periodic overdraft penalties, and time spent straightening out the mess they invariably make of their financial affairs. Firms that treat inventory records casually likewise pay a price: large buffer stocks, periodic production interruptions, premiums paid for rush reorders, and wasted management time. And, as we will see, the MRP[1] and JIT programs adopted by so many firms in recent years cannot hope to achieve their full potential when inventory records are unreliable.

WHAT ARE INVENTORY RECORDS?

Inventory records are hard copy or electronic documents that reflect how much and what kind of inventories a company has on hand, committed (allocated) to work-in-process, and on order. Just as a checkbook register is kept to tell us our balance at any given time without the necessity of going to the bank, these inventory records take the place of a laborious physical count every time we need to know our inventory status. And like a checking account, inventory levels are continually altered by purchases (deposits), allocations (checks outstanding), and sales (withdrawals and cashed checks written). The process is the same, but in the modern manufacturing firm, thousands of transactions may take place each day.

---

[1] MRP: a set of techniques that uses bills of material, inventory data, and the master production schedule to calculate requirements for materials. For additional sources of information see Darryl Landvater, *World Class Production and Inventory Management* (Essex Junction, VT; Oliver Wight Publications, 1993).

The Case of the Vanishing Best-Seller

A manager of a major New York book publisher was stunned by the reprint notice on his desk. It implied that he was almost out of stock on one of the firm's best-selling books. "Can't be," he thought. The monthly sales report indicated that there were 65,000 copies still in the warehouse. The firm used the *order point* inventory system to signal reorders of existing titles; that is, a reprint notice was generated and sent to the printer when the on-hand inventory balance reached a specified level—in the case of this book, 5,000 copies. The reprint quantity for this high-volume title was a whopping 100,000 units—not something you'd want to pile on top of an existing 65,000!

The publisher in question had a sophisticated and effective financial accounting system. With over 800 titles in print at any one time, and a continuous stream of individual books being shipped to and periodically returned from retail bookstores, it very effectively managed a complex burden of billings, credits, payments, and royalty statements. Errors were rare. Inventory accounting at the firm's several warehouses, however, did not operate with the same high level of precision: stock-outs of some titles and overstock of others were common, which made the manager immediately suspicious of the reprint order.

Sixty-five thousand books represented roughly 60 skids of packed cartons. The manager immediately called the warehouse manager, who responded, "All I have is 5,000. There's no way in hell there's an extra 60 skids of that title around here."

The manager insisted that they must be somewhere in the warehouse, and the next day he showed up at the warehouse door. With the warehouse manager who recruited two workers, they started combing the cavernous facility, which was about the size of a football field. Sometime around noon they found the missing 60 skids, which had been misidentified and placed in the back corner of the warehouse.

Had the manager not been so persistent, the firm would have generated an extra $300,000 worth of inventory.

Material is received in the stockroom and its receipt is recorded. The material is moved to its proper place in the stockroom, and this, too, is recorded. The next day the same material is moved to work center #1 for its first work-in-process step; and then on to work center #2, and so forth. When all work centers have finished with the material, it comes back to the stockroom. Each movement represents a transaction that is duly recorded. The following day, parts and materials are taken from the stockroom and sent to the assembly department, and those moves are recorded. When the assembly department has completed its work, the parts are moved back into stock, from which they are shipped to a customer and the sales order is closed.

By keeping accurate and complete records of each transaction, we know where and how much we have at every point in the process. Unfortunately, many companies do not maintain this level of inventory record accuracy. The result is confusion when accurate information is needed for making decisions on materials, production scheduling, marketing, and finance. These companies are forced to either make decisions based on questionable inventory records, or conduct time-consuming physical inventory checks before moving forward.

THE NEED FOR ACCURATE INVENTORY RECORDS

A company needs accurate inventory records for many reasons, the most basic of which is to create valid management plans.

Financial planning. An accurate statement of inventory assets, both on hand and on order, eliminates the need for periodic physical inventories, allows the CFO to better anticipate the need for short-term financing, and enhances the firm's ability to produce accurate and timely cash-flow and financial reports. Profitability—and thus taxes—is affected by inventories. It is not uncommon for companies projecting year-end profitability to be surprised and embarrassed by losses when physical inventories reveal wide discrepancies between inventory records and physical inventory counts.

Marketing and sales planning. An accurate statement of finished goods, item by item, not by dollars, is the best way to know exactly what can be sold to customers. Marketing plans can then be implemented to focus sales activity on specific products. (The most effective inventory reduction program ever devised is to sell existing inventory.)

New product planning. In many cases, a company's introduction of a new product renders one or more of its current products obsolete. To avoid many nonsalable older products and obsolete components, new product introductions are usually timed to roughly coincide with projected depletion of the old product inventory. Failure to keep accurate records makes this important timing impossible to finesse; the result is either premature introduction of the new product and lots of obsolete inventory left on hand, or a stock-out of the discontinued older product before its replacement is available for sale.

Procurement planning. If a company knows what it is going to make, when it is going to make it, and what inventory is on hand and on order, determining the quantity and schedule of future procurements is a simple calculation. The methodology utilized by most companies to perform these calculations is called Material Requirements Planning (MRP).

Production planning. An accurate statement of on-hand inventory allows a company to utilize its people and production facilities more fully because shortages can be predicted in advance of physically staging materials. This is another function commonly performed by MRP.

Just-in-Time (JIT) / Continuous Improvement (CI)[2]. These are powerful approaches to helping companies continuously improve their operations

---

[2] Just-in-Time has been defined as "the ongoing and relentless pursuit of the elimination of waste." It encompasses an ever-growing set of practices and techniques that firms are now employing to find and eliminate waste. The authors have noted that more and more practitioners are using a more descriptive term to articulate the implementation of those waste-reducing practices. The term is Continuous Improvement (CI). For this reason, Continuous Improvement is used throughout this book in place of JIT.

in the face of a more demanding competitive environment. A prime target of these programs is waste. Waste is defined as any activity that does not add value and can take the form of excess inventory, setup times, inspection, material movement, transactions, or rejects.[3] Implementation of JIT/CI programs can lead to dramatically lower inventories. Far from reducing concern for inventory accuracy, however, the need for accuracy actually *increases* with JIT/CI programs, as lower on-hand balances translate directly to a greater opportunity for stock-outs.

In companies actively pursuing JIT/CI programs, inventory stock-rooms are smaller or have been eliminated altogether in favor of "point of use" storage, and inventory balances are maintained through techniques called "backflushing." These issues will be addressed in Chapter 8.

Reduced need for physical inventories. Having accurate inventory records can also have a major impact on the time-consuming and ultimately wasteful process of taking physical inventories.

The modern manufacturing plant, with its dependence on high-cost equipment and skilled operators, must move at a tightly scheduled pace if it hopes to be competitive. But no matter how sophisticated its production scheduling, no matter how advanced its material planning, its elegant system is a house of cards if the underlying inventory record system is badly flawed.

U.S. Government requirements. In 1988, the U.S. government established ten Material Management and Accounting System Standards (MMASS) for federal contractors. Standard #5 requires contractors and subcontractors to "establish and maintain adequate levels of inventory accuracy" and affirms that "95% inventory record accuracy is desirable."

These are the more common purposes for which companies need the ability to create and maintain accurate inventory records. Others not listed here may be equally important to individual firms.

---

[3] William A. Sandras, Jr., *Just-in-Time: Making It Happen* (Essex Junction, VT: Oliver Wight Limited Publications, Inc., 1989), p. 9.

THE GOAL OF THIS BOOK

This book is intended as a step-by-step guide to creating and maintaining item-by-item inventory record accuracy of 95 percent or better to serve those previously mentioned purposes. It will thoroughly discuss the inventorying process, present the tools at the disposal of the materials management practitioner, and offer insights into how those tools can be effectively applied.

The core of the presentation is a three-phase approach to developing a solid inventory record system. The first of these phases is concerned with the design of the inventory record system and the creation of the internal capabilities to put it into place and keep it operating. The second phase is the straightforward development of initial inventory balances. The third and final phase is concerned with the ongoing operation and control of the inventory record system, one in which responsibilities are clearly delineated and in which the sources of errors can be located and eliminated.

Because of the importance of CI to so many inventory and industrial managers, an entire chapter is devoted to its requirements for record accuracy, and specific references to CI will be made throughout the text as appropriate. The chapters that follow will render full discussions of the following:

- The records a company should keep and how they should be kept

- Physical tools such as racks, scales, and bins

- Locating and addressing systems

- The transactions required to properly report and record events

- Timeliness of recording

- Demonstration of cycle counting techniques

- The correct way to take a physical inventory

- Details on the training needed to maintain high item-by-item inventory record accuracy

These tools have been applied successfully by small and large firms, in a wide variety of industrial settings. Whether a company is in a process industry, or is a batch manufacturer or job shop, with or without a stockroom, with or without paper transactions, the inventorying process is the same, and the concepts and tools discussed here are applicable.

Chapter Two

Tolerances and Measures of Accuracy

The assembly manager for Gizmo, Inc., was having a very good day until the production foreman came to tell her that his crew could not finish a particular customer order. "We need 500 widgets, part number 111," he said, "but we only have 200. We're short 300, and the stockroom is out. What do you want my crew to do until we can get more parts?"

The assembly manager quickly scanned the computer files for part number 111; the files clearly showed that 600 widgets were in stock. After walking back to the assembly line with the foreman, she checked the parts bin. There were the 200 he had mentioned. Her next stop was the stockroom, but the bin for this particular part was empty—again, just as the foreman had indicated.

"How can this be?" she wondered as she looked again at the computer terminal. As before, 600 were indicated as being on hand. Maybe a newly arrived order of the parts had been received but not yet entered into the computer. She trudged to the planning department, explained the situation, and asked if the parts were on order. The planner checked his computer terminal: "No, I haven't ordered any for weeks. I show 600 on hand."

The assembly manager knew that the lead time on this part was very long. She also understood that her people could not build more than 200 of the product until more parts arrived. With too few on hand and none on order, she would not be able to meet her production schedule on this product. Customer service would suffer. Revenue, too. And she would have to find something else for the assembly crew to work on while the planning department expedited an emergency order for the part.

Dozens of reasons were possible for the discrepancy between the inventory record and the actual situation in this case. Finding the source of the error could prevent future problems but would do nothing to improve the assembly manager's day. And certainly her trust in the accuracy of the inventory records would be guarded in the future. As we will discuss later, confidence in these records is essential.

Inventory records should be a mirror of what is actually happening in the store, on the factory floor, in the warehouse and stockroom, and with suppliers. If these records are inaccurate, it follows that decisions made from them will also be inaccurate.

Accurate inventory records not only prevent wasteful situations like the one above but also provide a company with the means to predict part shortages before they happen. To illustrate this, we need to consider the *fundamental manufacturing questions.* These are questions every manufacturer—of jet fighters, shoes, baked goods, paint, you name it— has to answer.

1. What are we going to make?

2. What does it take to make it?

3. What do we have?

4. What do we have to get, and when?

The Gizmo assembly manager had answered all of these questions, but inaccurate inventory records had led her into error on questions three and four.

MEASURING THE ACCURACY OF INVENTORY REPORTS

With the importance of inventory record accuracy to the smooth running of manufacturing operations firmly understood, we now need to clarify the meaning of accuracy.

Accuracy is not always absolute. First we need to understand that the term "accuracy" is used with a greater or lesser amount of precision. The expression "close enough for government work" humorously reflects this idea. We think of machined metal parts as being accurately made even though their dimensions may be slightly larger or smaller than exact design dimensions. Every machine produces these variances from specs, but as long as the parts do not deviate from the specs by more than a certain amount, we think of them as accurately made.

Every one of us drives down the highway on wheels that are imperfectly aligned to some extent. At 65 miles per hour we do not notice a minor misalignment. But a German driver hurtling down the autobahn at 120 miles per hour would certainly notice and no doubt demand a greater degree of accuracy in his wheel alignment.

In the ideal world, we would like everything absolutely perfect, but in reality, perfection is not necessary or achievable. Like machined parts and wheel alignments, inventory records in the manufacturing environment can be acceptable or accurate, without being perfect. This chapter addresses this issue along two important dimensions: measurement of inventory records, and the tolerances established to determine acceptable accuracy.

Measurement Techniques

There are many different techniques for measuring record accuracy. All require a comparison between actual quantities and recorded quantities. How well these quantities match determines, of course, the accuracy of the records. For an approach to measuring this match, consider Figure 2-1, which indicates the stock status for Gizmo, Inc.

This company's records show inventory of 100 each of 13 different parts. Someone has just taken a physical count which reveals a discrepancy between the actual count and the records for all but one part number. So how accurate or inaccurate are this company's records?

At first blush we would have to say that Gizmo's records are poor; in only one case have the records conformed to the physical count (part number 7). Strictly speaking, that is one out of 13—or a 7.7 percent—accuracy rate! But before we condemn this company, let's not forget

Figure 2-1   Measuring Inventory Accuracy

STOCK STATUS

GIZMO, INC.

P/N	Physical Count	Inventory Record	Tolerance (%)	Hit/ Miss	
1	94	100	± 2	X	
2	95	100	+ 5	X	
3	96	100	± 5	X	
4	97	100	± 2	X	
5	98	100	± 2	X	
6	99	100	± 2	X	
7	100	100	± 0	X	
8	101	100	± 0		X
9	102	100	± 5	X	
10	103	100	± 2		X
11	104	100	± 5	X	
12	105	100	± 5	X	
13	106	100	± 0		X
TOTALS:	1300	1300			

those inaccurately aligned wheels that most of us drove to work on today.

The *Tolerance* column indicates that Gizmo is willing to live with a small percentage variance from the inventory record on all but three part numbers. Thus, a *range* exists within which an actual value can miss the mark and the inventory record is still deemed *accurate*. For example, consider part number (P/N) 1 in Figure 2-1. If the record quantity for this part is 100 with tolerance of ±2 percent, its *acceptable range* is 98 to 102 (Figure 2-2). Therefore, if a physical count of P/N 1 is 98, 99, 100, 101, or 102, the record for P/N 1 is accurate—in our terms, a "hit." If the actual quantity was less than 98 or greater than 102, the individual part record would be inaccurate—a "miss." (With bulk measurements such as gallons, feet, or pounds, all physical measures between and including 98 and 102 are acceptable.)

Figure 2-2   Acceptable Tolerance Range

Inventory Record   =   100

Tolerance   =   ± 2%

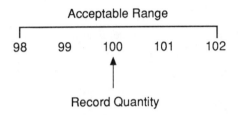

Acceptable Range

| 98 | 99 | 100 | 101 | 102 |

Record Quantity

A physical count within the range = An accurate record

Part Record Accuracy and Overall Inventory Record Accuracy

Since the physical count of P/N 1—94—indicates a "miss," the inventory record for this part is inaccurate. If this was the only part carried by the company, the company would have an inventory record accuracy of 0 percent. Fortunately, Gizmo, Inc., has a number of "hits" that bring up its average. P/N 2, for example, is an accurate part record. While only 95 of the recorded 100 parts are actually there, the tolerance of ±5 percent assigned to this part means that the actual count falls into its acceptable range (95 through 105).

We can measure the overall inventory record accuracy of a firm by means of a simple formula:

$$\text{Record accuracy} = \frac{\text{total accurate records}}{\text{total records checked}} \times 100\%$$

The sum of the accurate records divided by the sum of the records checked (both accurate and inaccurate) represents the *percentage inventory record accuracy*. In the case of Gizmo, a total of 8 accurate records out of 13 records checked results in 61.5 percent accuracy.

Problems with Dollarizing Inventory Records

Production and inventory personnel are not the only parties interested in inventory record accuracy. Financial managers take a lively interest in this subject—usually for quite different reasons. Financial managers need accurate inventory records so that they can establish an accurate dollar value for what is actually on hand. This value is essential when preparing periodic financial statements and determining profits, losses, and taxes. Both internal parties (management) and external parties (shareholders and tax authorities) are consumers of this information. Because of the need for accuracy in this dollar value, physical inventories are often taken.

In dollarizing inventory records, a value is assigned to each part. That value is multiplied by the number of pieces on hand for each part, and the sums for all parts are added together. The result is the total dollar value of all on-hand inventories.

An accurate dollarized inventory record is important but of limited value on the factory floor. The dollarized value of the firm's inventory could be accurate to the penny, but that accuracy could hide an appalling level of part-specific inaccuracy. To see how, consider again the inventory records of Gizmo (Figure 2-1). By a coincidence of our contriving, Gizmo—a company with a mediocre accuracy of 61.5 percent—has a physical parts count of 1,300 and an inventory record of 1,300. Again, strictly a coincidence. While these numbers match perfectly, Gizmo has too few of P/Ns 1 to 6 and too many of P/Ns 8 to 13. If each of these parts had a value of $1, the dollarized value of the physical count would exactly match the inventory record. There would be smiles all around in the finance and accounting departments. But down on the shop floor, production crews would be paralyzed by an overabundance of one part and a shortage of others. This paradox stems from the fact that money is interchangeable—"fungible," to use a more exact term. If your supplier is owed $100, you can pay him in all $1 bills or in combinations of many denominations. That works in the world of finance but not on the assembly line. If you are scheduled to assemble 50 automobiles and you have 80 left front fenders and 20 right front fenders, the fact that those fenders have the same dollar value will not help you. Likewise, two $40 gears are equal to one $80 carburetor on the company's balance sheet. In practice, the gears cannot be substituted for the carburetor or vice versa.

It should be noted that companies with high item-by-item inventory record accuracy (95 percent or better) always have exceptionally high fiscal inventory accuracy (99 percent plus) as well. Unfortunately, high fiscal inventory accuracy does not translate back to item-by-item accuracy. In fact, it is common for companies to have a fiscal accuracy in the 97 percent range and an item-by-item accuracy somewhere between 30 percent and 60 percent.

ESTABLISHING TOLERANCES

As we have seen, accuracy simply refers to how closely a feature conforms to a standard. That is, we measure a physical inventory balance by counting it and then compare that count to its record quantity (the standard). If they match, the record is accurate. If they do not, the record is inaccurate. We have also seen that we are often willing for practical reasons to "stretch" our definition of accuracy beyond an absolute number to a range of numbers through established tolerances. The Gizmo company has set tolerances on each of the part numbers in Figure 2-1. These vary from ±0 percent to ±5 percent. But why are there broader tolerances for some parts than for others?

Criteria for Setting Tolerances

Companies with outstanding inventory record accuracy and exceptionally productive operating systems have established tolerances as a function of a part's

- Usage

- Dollar value

- Lead time

- Level in the bill of material

- Criticality

- Method of handling

- Combinations of the above

As a rule of thumb, the higher the usage of a part, the greater the tolerance; that is, if the annual usage of a part is 100 per year, it might have a tolerance of ±0 percent (if this were the only consideration), while a part with a usage of 100,000 per year would probably be assigned a greater tolerance. And the higher the value, the tighter the tolerance; a part with a value of $10,000 would have a tolerance of ±0 percent, while a part with a value of $0.01 would likely have a greater tolerance. Thus, an aircraft manufacturer would likely have ±0 percent tolerance for jet engines—because of their high dollar value, long lead time to reorder, and critical importance to the final product—and a higher tolerance for rivets.

Most companies multiply usage by value in order to compute the dollars spent during the year for each part. The parts are then segregated into cost classifications using the Pareto Principle, which states that where there are a large number of contributors to a result, the majority of the result is due to a minority of the contributors. This is also known as the "80/20 rule," "the vital few versus the trivial many," and "ABC analysis." By following this principle, tolerances can be assigned as shown in Figure 2-3.

After computing the dollars spent per part, per year, a company would put this information in descending order. That is, at the top of the report would be the part on which the company spends the greatest dollar amount each year, and on down to the lowest dollar amount. Applying the Pareto Principle, approximately 20 percent of the parts

Figure 2-3   Tolerances By Cost Classification

Cost Class	Parts Purchased (% of Total)	Dollars Spent/Year (% of Total)	Tolerance (%)
A	20	80	±0
B	30	15	±2
C	50	5	±5

will represent 80 percent of the dollars spent by the company on inventory per year. These parts are referred to as the "A" cost class parts. Many companies start with a Pareto analysis to determine which tolerances to assign.[1]

There are many variations to this particular application. That is, "A" cost class parts may have a tolerance of ±1 percent, while the "B" cost class parts might have tolerances of ±1, 2, 3, or 4 percent. Regardless of the variations, the "A" parts normally have a tighter tolerance than the "B"s, which in turn normally have a tighter tolerance than the "C"s.

Although the ABC—or Pareto analysis—is helpful in assigning tolerances, it has limitations. As the usage of a part increases, it tends to move up the cost classification: "C" to "B" to "A," and thus its tolerance would tighten. This is directly opposed to the notion that as the usage increases, the tolerance should loosen. It is quite common to find that several "A" parts are actually low-cost, extremely high usage parts. For example, suppose an aircraft manufacturer uses 100 million rivets per year costing $0.10 each; the $10 million spent annually on rivets might push this low-priced part into an "A" cost classification. Of course, these are not the type of parts that a company would find economical to assign a ±0 percent tolerance.

The ABC approach also ignores the *lead time* of a part—a consideration when assigning tolerances. The longer the lead time, the tighter the tolerance. The logic behind this is quite simple: Responding to a stock-out situation is more difficult with a long lead-time part than with its opposite. Therefore, a tighter tolerance is required.

Another consideration for establishing tolerances is the level at which a part appears in the bill of material. Normally, the higher it is in the bill, the tighter the tolerance. A finished goods item is usually assigned a tighter tolerance than its components or raw material. This is quite obvious when rivets are compared to airplanes. However, this concept may not be applicable when the finished goods have low value and a high production volume such as ball point pens or razor blades.

---

[1] The Pareto Principle is discussed again in Chapter 7 with respect to establishing a priority order for cycle counting.

The *criticality* of a part to production, a company, or national defense is also a tolerance consideration. Parts that are proprietary to a new product's introduction, such as an integrated circuit based on new technology, would probably have a tolerance of zero. The same holds true for the so-called line stopper, top secret item, or critical item, such as the uranium isotope U235.

An extremely common method of assigning tolerance is the method of handling. If a part is discretely handled, that is, if it is counted into and out of stock one at a time, it is assigned a very low tolerance. On the other hand, when a part such as a common metal screw is scale-counted into and out of stock, it is usually assigned a tolerance greater than ± 0 percent but never greater than ± 5 percent. Contrary to past practice, this tolerance no longer represents the variability of the scales themselves but most likely represents the previously mentioned characteristics or inconsistent piece part weight. Companies tend to scale-count those parts with low value, high usage, low criticality, or are low in the bill of material. (Note: The exception to this discussion is the scale weighing of extremely high value items such as precious stones and metals and chemicals. A manufacturer of fine jewelry we visited weigh-counted *and* discretely counted all precious stones and metals; its inventory record accuracy was between 99 percent and 100 percent.)

A Great Sound and Fury with Marginal Benefits

Undoubtedly, other part characteristics could be used to establish tolerances for inventory accuracy. Analysts and consultants could spend days and weeks in either assigning tolerances to each part number or in developing a "system" to do this. However, excessive time spent in fine-tuning the assignment of inventory tolerances for particular parts has not shown itself to be time well spent. An informal study of firms whose personnel attended Oliver Wight Companies classes on inventory record accuracy and MRP II for middle management development over several years in the early 1980s showed that all of the above characteristics were in use. However, not all companies in the study used all the characteristics. Comparisons of accuracy between the companies using many to those using only a few showed no significant difference. In point of fact, many companies use ± 5 percent on all parts regardless of characteris-

The $20 Wager

Medieval theologians, apparently lacking more useful work, argued at length over such *esoterica* as the number of angels that could stand on the head of a pin, and the troublesome paradox that an all-powerful God might have the wherewithal to create a mountain so large that even He could not move it. They spent a lot of time thinking about these problems.

Similar cases of misdirected effort are observed today in the field of inventory record accuracy. Some people love to debate and analyze the tolerances set on particular parts when their energies should be directed to larger problems.

Several years ago, a stockroom manager named Sam was forced to attend our seminar on IRA. He was annoyed that his boss had required him to attend and was disturbed that anyone who had not personally been in his stockroom would presume to present methods on improving inventory records.

When the seminar instructor said "higher tolerances do little to improve measures of inventory record accuracy," Sam replied, "Says who?" The instructor responded that "this was indicated by a survey of hundreds of companies that have attended this seminar in the past." Sam fired back that if he could just broaden his tolerances to ±20 percent, his IRA percentage would go above 95 percent. He was clearly ready to debate the point all afternoon.

In an effort to move the seminar along, the instructor offered Sam this wager: "Sam, you stated your current IRA is 61 percent. I'll wager $20 that increasing your tolerances to ±20 percent won't get your IRA percentage to more than 70 percent."

Sam, who blamed his current tolerances of ±5 percent for his poor accuracy, accepted the wager.

A month passed, and the instructor had forgotten entirely about Sam until his phone rang one morning at 5:00 a.m. It was Sam (who lived several time zones east). "Send the $20, pal. I used ±20 percent tolerance and my IRA percentage has just hit 72 percent!"

The Sams of the business world spend too much time thinking about the wrong issues. Like mediocre tennis players, they think that if the net were lower they would score more "hits" and improve their game. The problem with their game, unfortunately, has little to do with the net and everything to do with other problems they are not addressing.

tics, and the productivity of their operating systems is no less than those that use a more comprehensive approach.

Quite simply, tolerance is not the issue that prevents companies from achieving and maintaining high inventory record accuracy. Thus, it follows that relaxing the tolerances will not lead to greatly improved record accuracy. It has been shown repeatedly that a large increase in tolerances (that is, increasing the acceptable range) makes only a slight increase in overall inventory record accuracy percentage. This was clearly illustrated at one company that reported 32 percent inventory record accuracy using a tolerance of ±5 percent on all parts. The company felt that this tolerance was too restrictive and that if the tolerance were relaxed, that is, to some number larger than ±5 percent, its accuracy would increase—an obvious conclusion. They were very surprised to find, however, that an increase in tolerance to ±20 percent increased their inventory record accuracy only from 32 percent to 40 percent.

When in Doubt Use ±5 Percent Tolerances

For companies unsure of what approach to follow, it is recommended that they start by assigning ±5 percent tolerance across the board on all parts, adjusting to a smaller percentage on an exception basis. This simple approach allows a company to get started without spending hours or days arguing over trivial matters. Additionally, the ±5 percent tolerance is extremely tight in comparison to practices found in most companies.

THE 95 PERCENT THRESHOLD

Experience in this area indicates that any company that has a 95 percent inventory record accuracy with ±5 percent tolerance on every item is in the top 10 percent to 20 percent of all manufacturing and distribution companies in the world with respect to inventory record accuracy. Furthermore, this 95 percent level of accuracy and maximum tolerance of ±5 percent on any part is an essential ingredient for any firm using either MRP II or CI. Ninety-five percent accuracy is not simply a recommendation but is a minimum *requirement* for these programs.

This has been determined through empirical studies by The Oliver Wight Companies at hundreds of companies that use formal planning and scheduling systems. Accuracy below 95 percent causes the performance of these systems to fall off dramatically.

One hundred percent accuracy is always the goal. Detailed surveys by The Oliver Wight Companies show, however, that 95 percent inventory record accuracy adequately supports formal planning and control systems.

The method for measuring inventory record accuracy presented in this chapter is simple and straightforward. One can devise fantastic statistical models to tackle the same problem. Most of these models, however, are more theoretical than practical. It has been our experience that they are also more confusing than helpful and that very few people actually understand them. Though some may be useful, simplicity remains the hallmark of true sophistication.

As presented, measuring accurate inventory records is basically a simple process, but it is only the first of many steps. In the chapter that follows, we will demonstrate the other steps a company must take to build a program that will allow it to both measure and maintain those records. They are steps that will allow any company to achieve the all-important level of 95 percent or better inventory record accuracy.

Chapter Three

The Three-Phase Approach to Inventory Record Accuracy

Now that the meaning of inventory record accuracy is clearly established, we turn our attention to the important and more difficult task of achieving the 95 percent accuracy level that forms the essential foundation of other manufacturing disciplines.

One company we know decided that its inventory records would improve by simply implementing a cycle counting program,[1] and did nothing to evaluate its current policies, procedures, and practices. In other words, it assumed that its current policies and procedures worked and that cycle counting would uncover all flaws in its processes. Theoretically, this would be true, but in practice this approach has important shortcomings. It may take months or years to identify all flaws in the process by this method. This particular company, in fact, used this method over a period of eight months, and its IRA percentage went from the low 50s to the mid-80s. This was an improvement, but it still lacked the accuracy needed to support Continuous Improvement or a formal planning and scheduling system such as MRP II. This company was advised to stop cycle counting, go back to square one, and utilize the three-phase approach discussed in this chapter.

---

[1] Cycle counting—explained in detail in Chapter 7—is a systematic approach to physically counting parts and materials on a regular basis.

Companies try many different approaches to achieve inventory record accuracy. All of them count all parts and materials, either with a physical inventory or with cycle counting, and wrongly assume that these periodic corrections of the inventory records will keep their records in close proximity to the reality of their on-hand balances. Few companies succeed with these limited panaceas. The point these companies miss is that unless their record-keeping process is capable of maintaining accurate inventory records, all the physical inventories and cycle counting in the world will not provide continued accuracy. Simply put, a flawed record-keeping process cannot maintain accurate records, but perform the process correctly, and you will have every opportunity to succeed.

Let us return briefly to our example of the bank checking account to see how process integrity is an essential ingredient of record accuracy.

The next time you go to your bank to transact business, pay close attention to what goes on inside the teller booth. When you step up to the teller window and initiate a transaction, the teller records the transaction in a manner that leaves nothing to chance. If you hand over $100 in cash with a deposit slip, the teller processes that transaction "by the numbers," that is, he or she counts the money, puts it into the cash drawer, enters a credit to your account, and issues a receipt to you and a copy to the bank. An electronic record is thus made of the transaction, and paper documentation is created to back up that record. At the end of the shift, the teller takes his or her cash drawer to a bank officer, who reconciles cash and checks in the drawer with backup documentation. If the amounts are off, the source of the error is pursued and corrected immediately. The bank has elaborately designed processes for dealing with the thousands of transactions that it handles each day, and it leaves nothing to chance or to the discretion of the teller or anyone else. That is why it works so well, and that is why most bank transactions can be handled by automated teller machines (ATMs). The process is so well designed and unambiguous that its steps can be readily programmed for smart machines. Within the bank, personnel are trained in the process, and a system of checks is used to assure that the process is working and that account records are accurate.

Imagine a situation in which the teller took your cash deposit and set it on the shelf or put it into his shirt pocket until after hours when he could document the transaction at a more leisurely pace. "Let's see now," he might ask hours later, "I think this $100 goes to George Brooks' account—but was it his savings or his checking?" Not our kind of bank. But this is how many companies handle their inventory records.

We offer a three-phase approach to improving and maintaining inventory record accuracy (see Figure 3-1). Each phase contains one or more tasks. If the tasks within each of these three phases is correctly implemented, inventory record accuracy of 95 percent or better is virtually assured.

PHASE I: DESIGN AND PREPARATION

This is the most important of the three phases for two reasons: it requires the greatest amount of thought and decision-making, and it is the firm foundation upon which the success of the subsequent phases rests.

In Phase I, the current operations of the company are analyzed and a set of working tools and procedures developed and tested. This phase designs the operational blueprint for day-to-day action on inventory-related activities. A system for creating and maintaining accurate inventory records is devised, just as banks did many years ago. Furthermore, personnel are trained to implement this operational blueprint.

This is the phase in which a company assesses what it currently has in place and establishes the policies and procedures necessary to make the process work over and over without fail. This phase normally takes six to twelve weeks to complete. Since the actual amount of time is directly related to the accuracy of a company's inventory records as it begins Phase I, companies that begin with grossly inaccurate records should expect to take more time.

PHASE II: ESTABLISHING INITIAL BALANCES

In contrast, Phase II is a one- to three-week job consisting of the rather straightforward business of establishing record balances, which is simply counting everything accurately. Chapter 6 discusses the flaws of the typical physical inventory and shows how to overcome them.

**Figure 3-1   Three-Phase Approach to Developing
Inventory Record Accuracy**

Phase I -   **Design and Preparation**
       1. Design Inventorying Process
           A. Stock vs Work-in-Process
           B. Layout
           C. Transactions
       2. Measure Starting Point
       3. Provide Tools
           A. People
           B. Systems
           C. Physical
       4. Finalize Policies and Procedures
       5. Train Personnel
       6. Education
       7. Assign Responsibility
       8. Implement New Policies and Procedures

Phase II -   **Develop Initial Balances**
       9. Develop Initial Balances

Phase III -   **Cycle Counting**
     10. Control Group Cycle Counting
     11. Ongoing Cycle Counting Program
           A. Select Method
           B. Assign Responsibilities
           C. Correct Error Causes

A systematic approach to establishing these balances that has been shown to yield accuracy very near 100 percent will be recommended.

PHASE III: CYCLE COUNTING

Cycle counting is the process of selecting a part to be audited, physically counting it, and comparing that count to the part's record count to determine record accuracy. We approach it in this final phase through both control group and ongoing cycle counting, and we show how these methods—which find and correct the source of errors—can be used to both maintain the accuracy of the records and eliminate the need for physical inventories. Since this phase is ongoing, it has no defined completion time.

THE ROAD TO INVENTORY RECORD ACCURACY

Before embarking on this course of improvement, many companies like to have some idea as to the likely course of their progress. Since so many firms have experience with the "learning curve" of operational progress, in which unit costs drop continually in a smooth curve, they naturally visualize their progress toward inventory record accuracy in similar terms, as graphed in Figure 3-2. Here the assumption is that the company begins with an inventory accuracy of 35 percent. Our experience with firms around the world indicates something quite different. By following the steps outlined in this book, the course of progress takes a stepwise path, as described in Figure 3-3. If we were to begin again at the 35 percent level, we would not see any upward movement during the first phase of our work.

Figure 3-2 Hypothetical Progress Toward Inventory Record Accuracy

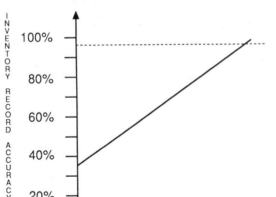

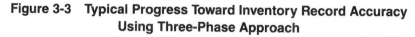

Figure 3-3   Typical Progress Toward Inventory Record Accuracy
Using Three-Phase Approach

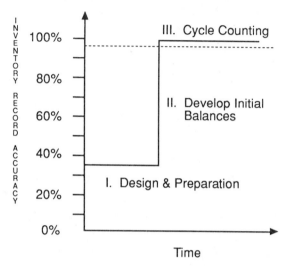

Then, during the second phase, inventory record accuracy would shoot straight up, rising above the 95 percent mark and then settling down[2] just above it.

The reasons for this stepwise progress lie in the nature of the three phases. As we have seen, Phase I is strictly a planning, designing, and training phase; as such, it will have no immediate impact on accuracy. Phase II, however, is an action phase in which all the records are recalibrated. Phase III is another flat period, but only because it is essentially one in which the progress already made is maintained.

NO TRICKS OR SHORTCUTS, JUST PLENTY OF HARD WORK

Any company pursuing this approach needs to realize that there are no shortcuts to success. The three-phase approach has been tried and

---

[2] Typically, record accuracy upon conclusion of Phase II is 99 percent to 100 percent. As routine activity (depositing and withdrawing of inventory) takes place in the stockroom, people make mistakes, and these mistakes count against record accuracy. The average IRA of companies diligently pursuing the three-phase approach discussed in this book will be between 95 percent and 99 percent.

proven in practice, but diligence and hard work have always been its companions.

It is extremely important that Phase I be completed before starting Phase II, and that Phase II be completed before starting Phase III.

Chapter Four

Design and Preparation Phase: Getting the System Right

"How do you eat an elephant?"

You may have heard this question before in regard to some large, formidable task. The answer, of course, is that you cut the elephant into small, manageable pieces and eat it one bite at a time.

Design and preparation is the largest of our three-phase approach, and so we have divided it into two manageable chapters.

In this chapter, we examine closely the inventorying process itself and present a model of that process. From this discussion, the way to design an inventory record system capable of 95 percent or better accuracy will be made clear. In the next chapter, we will address the people and policy aspects of the design and preparation phase.

UNDERSTANDING THE INVENTORYING PROCESS

Manufacturers have been trying for years to lower unit costs of their products through automation and other productivity-enhancing efforts. Most of these high-minded efforts have been costly mistakes. Only after many, many failures have they looked closely at their processes and discovered that the upper limits of their cost reductions are *predetermined* by the product design; an estimated 70 percent of manufacturing unit cost is now thought to be locked into the design itself. Thus, the greatest opportunities to improve unit manufacturing costs are found within improved design. This is why so many manufacturers are re-designing their products to eliminate cost-incurring machining, assembly, and finishing steps at the designer's table. The same applies to inventory record accuracy. The inventorying process is at the heart of an accurate record system. How this process is designed determines the level of accuracy it is capable of achieving. What could be more logical?

Unfortunately, most companies spend little time designing this process. They make the mistake of thinking that because they have existing inventory forms, policies, and procedures, merely doing a better job with these items will improve inventory accuracy. But no amount of dedication will redeem an inventory system that is flawed at its core. These companies need to find the real *driver* of record accuracy, and that driver is embodied in the inventorying process itself. It is at the heart of creating and maintaining accurate inventory records.

Simply stated, the inventorying process includes the receiving of parts, putting them away, and their storage, withdrawal, issue, and movement through work-in-process while simultaneously tracking their movement and maintaining records of those events and their effects.

Record accuracy is the product of the inventorying process. Again, most companies spend little time designing this process because they assume it is already in place and working well, which can be a critical error when implementing an inventory record accuracy improvement program. The practitioner should make the assumption that the process is faulty and examine it closely to uncover shortcomings. Only after this examination has been made, and the process ascertained as capable of maintaining 95 percent accuracy, should the next steps in an accuracy improvement program be undertaken.

As practitioners we were continually perplexed by the difficulties that surrounded the maintaining of accurate inventory records. The problems for those directly responsible for that job always seemed embedded in the minutiae of the outer dimensions of the process. They would talk for hours about contract and account numbers, problems linked to the union, the finance system, voucher numbers, and purchasing and manufacturing orders. These concerns quite clearly distracted them from the fact that their inventorying process itself was the source of their problems and inaccuracies.

Figure 4-1 is a model of the inventorying process. It has two parts. The first part is a physical movement process representing how material moves into and out of stock and provides us with a physical quantity on hand. This part of the model is like the stockroom: Material is physically brought in (by hand, truck, pipeline, and so forth); it is also physically removed. What is physically left—the residual—is the actual on-hand quantity.

The record-keeping process is the other half of the model. It is an arithmetical reflection of the physical movement process. It is maintained on either a manual or a computerized file. Whenever material physically moves into or out of stock, that movement is mirrored as a *transaction* in the record-keeping process. A transaction in this system is either an "in" or an "out." An "in" increases stock; an "out" decreases it. We can increase stock in just a few ways: by receipt (as from purchasing), by a return to stock from work-in-process, or by some upward stock adjustment. Stock is decreased by issuing it (to customers and/or to work-in-process), by scrapping it, or by a downward stock

Figure 4-1 The Inventorying Process

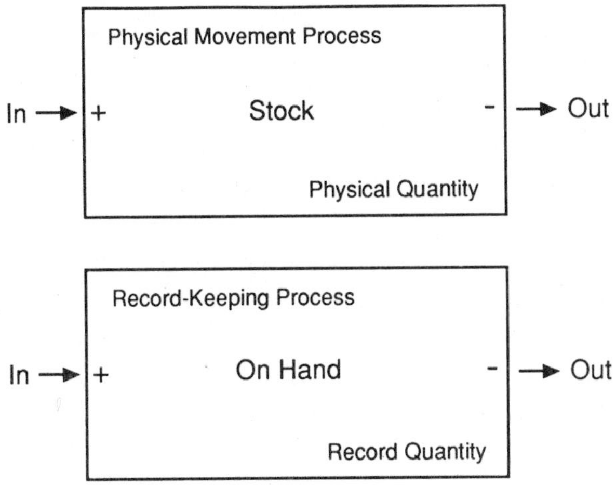

adjustment. (Note: In this chapter we use the terms "stock" and "on hand" on an interchangeable basis.)

A properly designed inventorying process is one that is capable of producing a match between these physical and transaction events, in which the physical "stock" quantity exactly equals the "on-hand" record quantity.

If at any point during Phase I there is uncertainty as to whether or not to record a material movement, use Figure 4-1 as a litmus test. Think of the record-keeping process (bottom of figure) as a mirror of the physical movement of materials (top of figure). The actual movements of material are the events that need to be recorded.

THE WORK-IN-PROCESS (WIP) MODEL

The inventory that we physically moved into stock back in Figure 4-1 will not stay there forever. In a retail firm, which simply marks up the price of its inventory and offers it for sale, stock moves rapidly and is sold shortly after receipt. Incoming stock for a manufacturer, however, undergoes some transformation before this happens because manufacturing is a value-adding activity. Steel I-beams and plates are cut, drilled, and welded to become truck trailers. Cotton is dissolved in solvents and becomes film dope, which in turn becomes celluloid for photographic film. These parts leave their stock status for a new status—work-in-process[1]—and eventually come back to stock as different products. Each movement into and out of stock needs to be captured in the inventory record system.

The work-in-process, or shop floor, of most manufacturing companies can be categorized as batch, process, or Continuous Improvement environments (or some combination thereof). Regardless, the design of the inventorying process is essentially the same, that is, practitioners must understand and record how material flows in, through, and out of the facility. However, the authors realize that CI environments have some special requirements, and these are addressed in Chapter 8.

---

[1] Work-in-process inventory is also known as W.I.P., WIP, whip, and in Canada and the United Kingdom, work-in-progress.

The inventorying process model shown in Figure 4-1 is concerned only with stock inventory. It is synonymous with "on hand" or "in stock." This stock inventory is not being worked on; there is no value-adding activity. To visualize that activity, we offer Figure 4-2. Here work-in-process is added to stock as a loop connecting the right and left ends of the box. This shows how the two types of inventory—stock and WIP—relate to each other within the material planning and control system of Material Requirements Planning.

Figure 4-2   Stock Versus WIP (Within MRP)

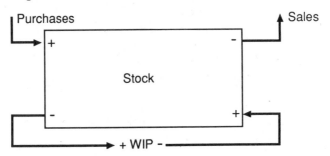

Note the "plus" and "minus" signs at the points in the model at which transactions take place. When purchases are brought into stock, stock increases (+); stock is reduced (−) when it goes to sales. Likewise, when components go out to the factory floor as WIP, stock is reduced and WIP is increased. When the value-adding activities are completed, the parent part comes back into the stockroom from WIP, stock is increased, and WIP is reduced. It is a double-entry form of transactional accounting in which an increase here is a decrease there.

WIP, like stock, can be increased or decreased in only a handful of specific ways. It can be increased when something is issued to it from stock. It can be decreased when work is complete and a parent part is received into stock.

Figure 4-3 helps us to better understand the WIP model. This represents a bill of material, a recipe for adding value to some stock part by means of the WIP loop. In this case, the part to be created is number 1100. To get this part, we must start with part 3300, perform some sawing, turning, and grinding to get part 2200—an intermediate product; this must be ground, plated, and polished to obtain our 1100.

Figure 4-4 presents a model of the inventorying process for this activity in which one part 3300 is procured on a purchase order and no items are on hand as stock. In Figure 4-5, part 3300 is received into stock.

In a traditional environment, a manufacturing order[2] (MO) would

Figure 4-3   Bill of Material

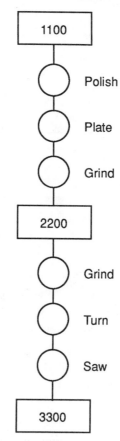

<hr />

[2] In this book, the term "manufacturing order" is synonymous with "work order," "shop order," and so forth.

Figure 4-4   Part on Order, None in Stock

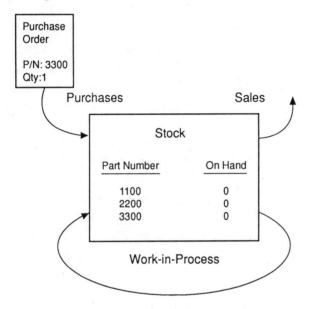

Figure 4-5   Part 3300 Received in Stock

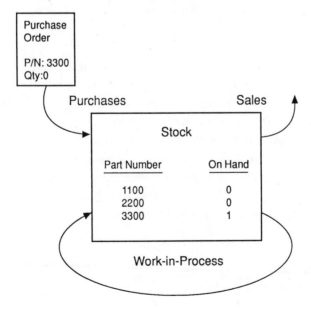

then be created for part 2200. This authorizes the withdrawal from stock of part 3300 (per the bill of material) and the value-adding steps described therein. When that happens, part 3300 is technically issued out of stock and into the WIP loop (Figure 4-6). Once the value-adding operations have been performed on part 3300, it has been converted into its parent, part 2200. According to the record, this technically takes place when the manufacturing order for part 2200 is received into stock from WIP (Figure 4-7).

Now, halfway toward the finished product, a manufacturing order is created for part 1100. This authorizes the withdrawal from stock of part 2200 and the value-adding activities. When part 2200 is withdrawn from stock and issued to the manufacturing order for part 1100, part 2200 technically moves out of stock and into WIP (Figure 4-8). When the value-adding steps have been done, 2200 has been physically converted into 1100. According to the record, this takes place when the manufacturing order for part 1100 is received into stock from WIP (Figure 4-9).

The bill of material described in Figure 4-3 is represented in Figure 4-10 with added terminology. Note that 1100, 2200, and 3300 have been labeled as "part numbers." Also, each has been labeled "parent," "parent/component," or "component."[3]

Part Levels

Each part is also assigned a "level" in the bill of material—the top being 0. There is no limit to the number of levels a bill of material can have. The value-adding steps between these levels are called operations; they are not assigned part numbers. Note that in the manufacturing process, the piece of material that began as part 3300 went through the WIP loop twice: first as a component, then as a component/parent. To determine how many times any part must pass through this loop on the way to becoming a 0-level parent part, simply locate its level number. This number indicates the number of times it must go into and out of WIP.

---

[3] A component is any part that will be transformed into something else. A parent is any item that is made from the component(s). A part can be both a parent and a component (part 2200).

Figure 4-6   Part 3300 Moves to WIP

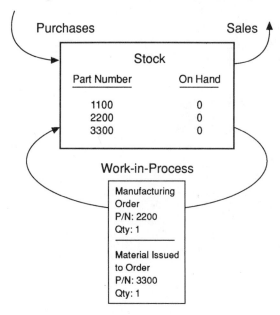

Figure 4-7   Part 2200 Moves into Stock from WIP

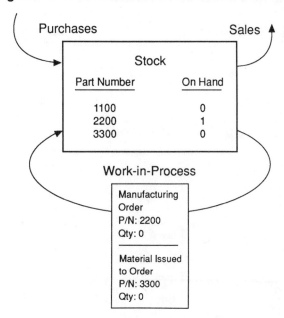

Figure 4-8   Part 2200 Moves Back to WIP

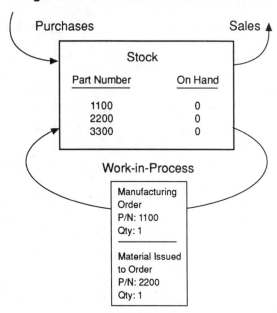

Figure 4-9   Part 1100 Moves to Stock from WIP

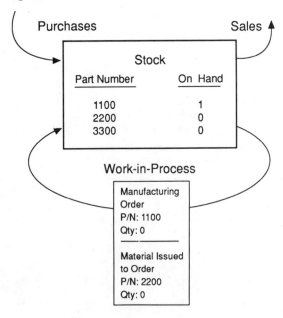

Figure 4-10   Revised Bill of Material

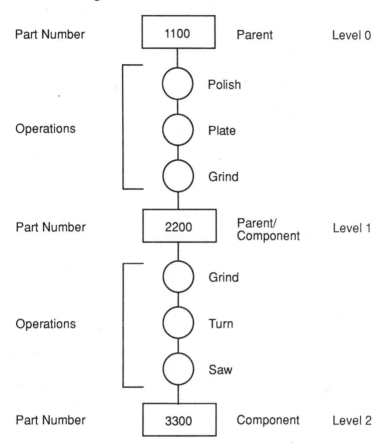

Part Numbers and Stock

One useful point of distinction between stock and WIP worth noting here is that any material in stock must have a part number assigned to it. Materials in WIP are between part numbers. They are no longer components but are not yet parents. Referring back to Figure 4-10, we observe part 2200, the parent, can be in stock since it has a part number. Part 3300, the component, likewise can be in stock. However, component 3300 cannot be in stock after it has been through the turning operation because it is no longer component 3300 and is not yet parent 2200. The manufacturing steps between this parent and component represent work-in-process, which we track with the manufacturing order to make the parent.

Work-in-Process Starts and Ends at Stock

WIP always starts from stock and ends at stock (see Figure 4-2). For users of MRP principles in particular, this is an extremely important point to remember. Physically, it is possible to purchase a component and move it directly into WIP. This is not possible, however, if a record is to be made of it. MRP insists that it must first be received in stock and then issued to WIP. This is also true for a manufactured item.

Work-in-Process as Finance Sees It

It is important to realize that finance uses the term WIP in a different context than MRP. This distinction is worthy of explanation because it is a frequent source of confusion.

Traditionally, the financial staff of a manufacturing company acts under the assumption that the firm buys material—bar stock or completed truck engines—to be converted into finished products, such as delivery trucks, through a value-adding process. It refers to these purchases as "raw material." When some, but not all, of the value has been added, that inventory becomes WIP in the eyes of finance. That WIP inventory is commonly found on the factory floor or in the semifinished or subassembly stockroom. When the last increments of value are added, that inventory is called *finished goods* (Figure 4-11).

As noted earlier, when a formal planning and control system such as MRP is employed, the distinctions between raw materials and work-in-process, and work-in-process and finished goods are different. MRP distinguishes between inventory types based more on location and commitment to the value-adding process than on its stage of manufacture. Specifically, MRP recognizes only two types of inventory: stock and work-in-process. It is either one or the other. Even when the final manufacturing processes are finished, it comes back into stock. Figure 4-12 shows the application of these two viewpoints to our bill of material through its several levels and manufacturing operations.

Only after flow of materials is firmly understood—from purchases to

Figure 4-11   Finance Versus MRP II

Finance	MRP II
Raw Material	Stock
WIP	WIP
	Stock
Finished Goods	Stock

stock, from stock directly to sales, from stock to WIP and back again as transformed parts, and from stock to sales—can the inventorying process that is capable of maintaining accurate inventory records begin to take shape. But other aspects of inventory transactions remain to be addressed.

ALLOCATIONS

Allocations are reservations for parts that have not yet been withdrawn or issued from stock. Nevertheless, they are spoken for in some sense and are thus not available. Generally speaking, allocations belong to sales orders or manufacturing.

Sales Orders

In a catalog sales operation, a customer's order is taken over the telephone by a customer service representative who enters the SKUs, (SKU = Stock Keeping Unit) ordered into an on-line order entry system. This is done by first establishing a sales order number. The SKUs are added to the sales order as separate lines or "line items." Taken together, the line items make up the entire order. The line items allocate, or reserve, inventory for this specific sales order. They do not reduce the current

Figure 4-12   Bill of Material as Seen by Finance and by MRP

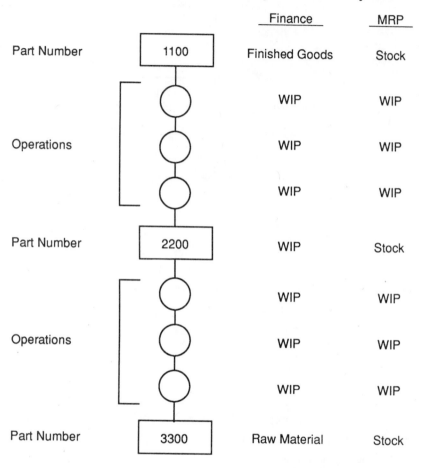

		Finance	MRP
Part Number	1100	Finished Goods	Stock
	○	WIP	WIP
Operations	○	WIP	WIP
	○	WIP	WIP
Part Number	2200	WIP	Stock
	○	WIP	WIP
Operations	○	WIP	WIP
	○	WIP	WIP
Part Number	3300	Raw Material	Stock

on-hand quantity but merely put some of it on hold. This, in effect, reduces the *available* inventory, which is on-hand inventory less allocated inventory.

As an example, let us suppose that you picked up the phone and called Down East Outfitters, Inc., to order two pairs of men's fire engine red suspenders. The customer service rep would ask you for the catalog number of this item (SKU), then quickly check the screen for available inventory. It might appear like this:

#10-332-2, Men's Suspenders, Red

On-hand inventory	20
Allocated inventory	5
Available inventory	15

Seeing that 15 are currently available, she would confirm that fact to you and enter your sales order for 2 sets of suspenders, the sales order would in turn, allocate the appropriate inventory. That transaction would increase allocated inventory to 7 and decrease available inventory to 13. On-hand inventory would remain the same at 20. Only when any of the allocated inventory items are issued from stock, and so reported with a transaction, would on-hand inventory decrease; (allocated inventory would be simultaneously decreased).

This allocated inventory mechanism, teamed with a real-time data system, makes it possible for the customer rep to "reserve" inventory items for sale on a first-come, first-served basis and prevents the selling of depleted inventory items. If all red suspenders were already allocated at the time of your call, the customer service rep would tell you so and ask if you would be willing to wait for their next shipment.

Your checkbook provides a useful analogy to this process. When writing a check and presenting it to a merchant for some purchase, you enter the amount into the check register. This, in effect, allocates those funds to the merchant. The funds are still on hand in the bank and remain there until the check is presented for payment by the merchant. Recording the check in the register helps you avoid spending the same funds twice and allows you to calculate funds available for other purchases.

Obviously, on-hand inventory can be reduced directly at the moment of order entry without the need for this allocation device, but this can produce problems. By reducing inventory at order entry, cycle counting becomes very difficult; that is, the record on-hand balance is reduced before the physical inventory is removed from stock. By our earlier definition, this would be a flaw in the design of our system because the physical count and the record count would be different.

Manufacturing Orders

Manufacturing orders can produce allocations in exactly the same way but through bills of material. This is particularly helpful when the parent part, such as a television set, is made of dozens or hundreds of components. When a manufacturing order (MO) is created for a parent part, the MRP system references the bill of material for the parent and multiplies each required component by the quantity specified by the MO. Figure 4-13 illustrates this for a parent that has two different components. The MO calls for making five of part number 3600. Each of these five parent parts is made from one part 3700 and two of part 3800. The MRP system calculates the total allocations.

Allocations are MO specific; they are linked to the MO that creates them. Thus, a convenient way to visualize allocations is as buckets attached to a specific MO. Each bucket (allocation) is labeled to hold a specific component as stated in the bill of material. Each bucket is also sized to the exact number of components required by the bill of material and the MO. Figure 4-14 shows these component buckets attached to its manufacturing order, with the specified quantity indicated. The bucket for part number 3800 is filled (10), while that of part number 3700 is not (4 of 5).

Figure 4-13   Allocation Produced by Manufacturing Order

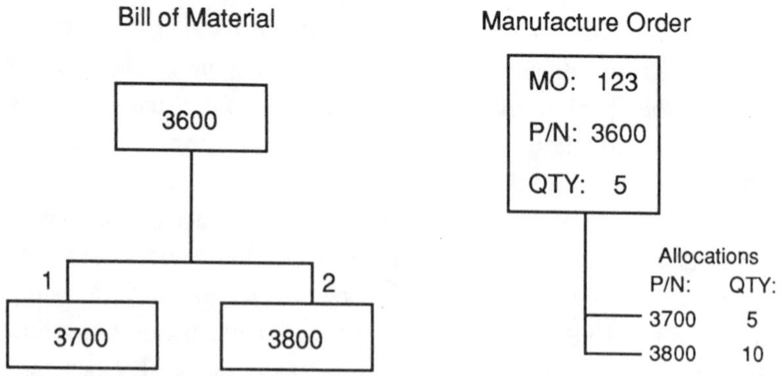

Bill of Material   Manufacture Order

Keeping track of work-in-process is relatively easy once allocations are understood. Manufacturing order 123 should be out on the factory floor. Per inventory records, 4 P/N 3700 and 10 P/N 3800 are with it. As this MO moves from work center to work center, the buckets and their contents will move with it. The inventory record for P/N 3700 shows an open (unsatisfied) allocation owed to MO 123 for 1 P/N 3700. This is also called a "shortage" and would signal an action message to a material planner that supply and demand were out of balance.

TRANSACTIONS

Transactions are necessary to record events. When your banker honors the check you wrote to the mortgage company, it is recorded as a transaction. When the stockroom fills a manufacturing order for 200 of P/N 3900, that, too, is recorded as a transaction. In manufacturing and distribution companies, transactions are the vehicles we use to record specific material movements.

Transactions for inventory reports should not be complicated or confusing. Nor need there be many different types. At a minimum, there are two: into and out of stock. Few companies, in our experience, need more than seven different kinds of inventory transactions, and all of them are

Figure 4-14   Allocation Buckets

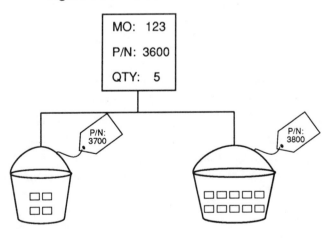

forms of "ins" and "outs" we have already encountered. This basic set includes the following:

- Planned[4] receipt

- Planned issue

- Return to stock

- Unplanned receipt

- Unplanned issue

- Stock-to-stock transfer (moving material from one stock location to another)

- Inventory adjustment (increase or decrease)

- Scrap

Figure 4-15 shows the effects that each of these transactions has on the inventory records. It is important to note that in each case the effects on all records occur simultaneously. Thus, when a planned receipt is made, the on-hand record is increased and the on-order record is simultaneously decreased. When a stock-to-stock transfer is made, the location that receives the material increases its record, and, at the same time, the sending location decreases its record.

Transaction Flows

In a large organization, one with multiple stockrooms, many storage areas, plenty of work-in-process, and thousands of separate part numbers on hand and on order at any one time, designing an inventory record system that is manageable and capable of maintaining accurate records is no small task. Transactions take place at a rate that even bankers would find daunting. We have just scratched the surface on some of the thorny

---

[4] The term "planned" has to do with the material planning system. For example, a planned issue is one that has been anticipated. An unplanned issue would be an issue not anticipated, such as an emergency demand.

Figure 4-15 Transactions and Their Effects on the Records

	On Hand	Allocations	On Order (Purchased)	WIP
Planned Receipt:				
From WIP (Parent)	+			-
From Suppliers	+		-	
Planned Issue to WIP (Component)	-	-		+
Planned Issue to Customer	-	-		
Return to Stock from WIP (Component)	+	+		-
Unplanned Receipt	+			
Unplanned Issue	-			
Stock to Stock Transfer	- & +			
Inventory Adjustment	- or +			
Scrap from WIP (Component)				-
Scrap from Stock	-			

issues that need attention. On the positive side, however, practitioners can form as many IRA improvement teams as there are stockrooms.

Regardless of the size of the stockroom or the company's material flow, one thing that must be done to gain mastery over this otherwise uncontrolled system is to map out the flow of inventory and the types of transactions that can occur. Figure 4-16 is just such a map, drawn for an actual manufacturing company. This flowchart serves a number of important purposes:

1. It forces the practitioner to think through all situations when designing the inventorying process.

2. It defines how materials flow through the facility.

3. It defines what transactions will be required to move materials.

4. It can be used to train employees.

5. When enlarged, it can be displayed prominently throughout the company to serve as a transaction reference guide.

Figure 4-16 Inventory Locations/Transactions
(Batch Environment)

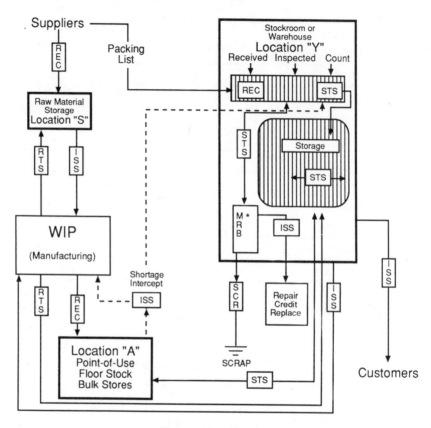

Transaction Key

REC - Receipt

ISS - Issue

STS - Stock-to-Stock Transfer

RTS - Return to Stock

SCR - Scrap

*MRB - Material Review Board

A transaction flowchart provides a handle on how things are supposed to work within a company and provides guidelines to the design of the inventorying process.

It is imperative for someone to do this if only to define what is "right." Lacking a definition of what is "right," everyone in the system is free to make his or her own interpretation—with potentially disastrous results for inventory record accuracy.

A good way to get started is to simply draw four boxes on a flip chart: one each for suppliers, stock, work-in-process, and customers. Then chart the flow of materials. For example, material is issued from stock to WIP, so draw a line from stock to WIP. Put an issue transaction symbol there to capture this event. Continue on to all the other transactional locations. The result should be a graphic representation of how material moves into, through, and out of the facility, and a demonstration of where and what transactions occur.

This accomplished, the chart should be professionally drawn and reproduced. Copies should be displayed in the stockroom, the receiving areas, throughout the work-in-process areas, and on the shipping dock to provide everyone with a quick reference as to what types of transactions are required at any given point. More important, the chart defines correct practice, and that is the basis for both ongoing activity and training.

SOFTWARE CONSIDERATIONS

Computer technology and transaction-recording jobs were made for each other. It is no coincidence that bookkeeping, customer statement records, and other forms of tabulation were among the first to become computerized. Today, there are many inventory applications and materials management software programs available: either off the shelf or custom-tailored to the specific needs of individual firms. Few companies of any size operate without them.

A company needs to take a number of factors into consideration regarding the software it uses. Many of the factors companies use to select materials management software go beyond the scope of maintaining accurate inventory balances. However, every software package comes with data filters, barriers, and edits. These built-in tools are used to check every transaction before it is accepted into the record. Companies that write their own software are advised to include these tools in their systems. The important ones are the following:

1. The system should edit all transactions and recognize only legitimate transaction codes.

2. It must assure that all required data fields are completed.

3. The system should flag any illegitimate part or order numbers.

4. The software must be capable of matching part numbers to schedules or order numbers and reject transactions for which numbers do not match.

5. It should flag mismatches and request a correction.

A more subtle capability to look for in software is the ability to test for "reasonableness." This checks such things as the quantity of receipts and issues to determine if they fall within logical ranges. For example, if an issue transaction were to cause an on-hand balance to become negative, it would be rejected for correction. Many firms operate with software that would show a negative on-hand balance if certain transactions were fed into the system. Since we cannot have negative on-hand balances, programs like these fail the test of reasonableness.

CONCLUSION

We know from experience with many companies that there are only two reasons for a failure to achieve inventory record inaccuracy: The first is some fault within the system, and the second is someone not doing his or her job.

In this chapter, we focused our attention on the system. If we do a poor job on its design, no amount of hard work and people doing their jobs will result in a minimum of 95 percent inventory record accuracy. But if we design it correctly, the paper and electronic counting of the system will be a faithful reflection of what is really on hand, allocated, or on order. We are looking for a process that meets the design criteria of being simple, transparent, and reflecting reality. At that point our energies can be turned to the business of training and managing the people who make the system work. We address that task in the next chapter.

Chapter Five

Design and Preparation Phase: The Physical Stockroom

A man entered a bank in which he had a $100,000 account. He walked up to a teller window, put his hand across the counter and into the money drawer, and extracted a few hundred-dollar bills. Suddenly, he found himself surrounded by employees and security guards. He explained that since he had $100,000 in the bank, he should have physical access to those funds; a bank officer politely explained why that cannot be allowed and why limited access to the teller's cash drawer helps assure the accurate safekeeping of his funds.

Few of us need to be told why we cannot just reach into the teller's cash box to withdraw our bank funds, yet few in the manufacturing workplace recognize the need for the same restrictions to assure the integrity of their company's working assets. For many workplaces, in our experience, the stockroom is a convenient shortcut to the parking lot; a clean and quiet spot to take a lunch break; or a place to rummage for components when one on the assembly line is defective.

Firms that expect to achieve and maintain accurate inventory records need to instill a set of stockroom-related attitudes, disciplines, and procedures in support of the design of transactions already discussed. The most well designed inventory record system in the world will not produce 95 percent accuracy if stockrooms are not secure, if employees are not trained to run a tight ship, and if no particular person has the ultimate responsibility for that accuracy. By contrast, banks not only have well-designed systems to record and account for every dollar of "inventory," they also have formal procedures as to who can be in the vault and the tellers' cages. Tellers are accountable for the accuracy of their cash balances on a daily basis, and a bank officer, the cashier, has responsibility for all discrepancies. There is a formal break-in period for new employees, job descriptions are very specific, and procedures are well documented. The result is a level of accuracy that exceeds 99 percent.

This chapter continues our discussion of the design and preparation phase for instituting an inventory process capable of maintaining accurate records. It begins with the measurement of the existing records to form a baseline against which future progress can be gauged. The focus then turns to the security and layout of the stockroom. This leads naturally to the very significant problem of tracking the location of parts within and outside the stockroom. In ending this discussion, we will turn to the importance of education, training, and the assigning of responsibility for accurate inventory records.

MEASURING THE STARTING POINT

We already know where we want to be with our inventory records: at least 95 percent accurate. Few in management or in the stockroom will disagree with that objective. Even fewer will agree about the current state of their company's record accuracy. In our experience, we have found it important to take a baseline measure of inventory record accuracy at this point in the design and preparation phase. This makes it clear to everyone, including the doubters, just how much work needs to be done.

Once the decision has been made to embark on an accuracy improvement program, it is important not to waste a great deal of time measuring a large sample of inventory records. A small sample will do very well. Our recommendation is to choose 50 parts at random in the stockroom, count them, and compare that figure to the inventory record balances. Then choose another 50 parts at random from the inventory records and compare these record balances to the actual physical balances in the stockroom. Here again, time spent debating tolerances for this small sample is time wasted. Use ±5 percent on all parts but keep the raw data. The combined accuracy of all 100 parts is then a starting point. It is important to choose this sample from both the records and the actual physical balances because it is possible for a part to be physically in the stockroom but not reflected in the record. The opposite is also true. The record could, in fact, reflect an on-hand balance while the stockroom contains none. By choosing the sample in the manner described, both errors will be uncovered.

Once this number has been determined, make sure that all those involved in the inventorying process know what it is. This "before" snapshot will then provide a sense of purpose as they move forward, and a source of satisfaction as they look backward from a point of improved accuracy.

THE PHYSICAL STOCKROOM

The mechanics of the inventorying process demand that certain procedures be in place and that we use the right tools to get the job done. As stated earlier, this process begins by establishing limited access.

Limited Access

The definition of limited access is that *only* those people are allowed in who have a business purpose in the stockroom. Traditionally, this has meant that certain physical barriers need to be erected: fenced stockrooms or stockrooms physically detached from the manufacturing facility. In the minds of some, limited access still means a fifteen-foot chain-link fence topped by concertina wire, with a junkyard dog and a security guard for good measure. Our concern is less with physical barriers, however, than with mental barriers. We want to create a situation in which the stockroom is viewed as a special place where special rules of behavior apply. The "quiet" sign in a hospital zone is not a physical barrier to noise, but it is universally respected as a guide to behavior. The dog for whom the living room is "off limits," even though it is not gated off, is not restrained by a physical barrier but by instilled training.

The Stockroom Rambo

Stockrooms can be secured with walls and padlocks, and these will solve some of the problems of limited access, but a company-wide attitude that respects the integrity of the stockroom, and that differentiates parts that are available for use from those that are not, is ultimately much stronger. And that attitude must start at the top. As an example, consider a case in which a production supervisor was faced with a true dilemma: violate the integrity of the stockroom and its record system or watch his company miss an important shipping deadline.

Almost everyone had left for the annual company picnic on the Friday before Memorial Day, leaving only a skeleton crew to put the finishing touches on a complex and expensive mechanical system, which had to be shipped by that evening. Failure to ship that evening would put the company in default on a contract specification and result in a substantial financial penalty. One final quality assurance test caused a hydraulic component to fail. Its only replacement was under lock and key in the new-product stockroom.

There was no question in this production supervisor's mind that he was going to ship the product that evening. The only decision was how to get the replacement component. The key to the new-product stockroom was locked in the desk of the new-product manager, who was assumed to be at the picnic and out of touch. Perhaps they could break into his desk to get the key. Another possibility was to cut the chain on the storeroom door and then relock the cage. That, in fact, was the supervisor's choice. As he approached the door with a cutting torch, his audience, the skeleton crew, began to cheer him on. The symbolism of this action—violating company rules to advance the company's own interests—was just too powerful to suggest half measures, so instead of just cutting the chain, the supervisor cut the *entire door* off the new-product storeroom. He helped himself to the hydraulic component, put it on the unit, and shipped it that night. But even as the door fell from its hinges, to the great applause of his crew, the supervisor had an uncomfortable feeling that he would not be a hero but a man in deep trouble.

As the supervisor relaxed at home that evening, his phone rang. Plant security had tracked him down. Then came the call from the new-product manager, who was furious. The supervisor's own boss called and was livid. It looked as though he *was* in deep trouble.

No sooner had our supervisor arrived at the plant on Tuesday morning than the loudspeaker began paging him to report to the CEO's office. Everyone in the plant knew why he was heading to the office, and speculation about his fate was running at a high level. But as he walked into the CEO's office, the supervisor knew that he would be the hero and not the goat.

The CEO was sitting behind his desk; the supervisor's boss was standing next to him; and on the other side was the regional vice president of the customer whose order had resulted in the entire episode. All three had Cheshire cat grins on their faces.

"Son," the CEO said with his hand now extended, "if I had seventeen more purebred SOB's like you, we'd do nothing but ship product." The customer chimed in that he "just wanted to meet the guy who made it all happen."

Our supervisor was suddenly a hero. But the firm's control over access to its stockrooms was the loser from that day forward. The supervisor should have been disciplined for violating the limited access rule, which would have clearly established unacceptable behavior with respect to limited access. Instead, his behavior was sanctioned and rewarded by the CEO. He received the largest year-end bonus of his peer group.

In some companies, even fences and padlocks are not enough to establish limited access to storeroom assets; in other companies, those whose managements support the ethic of limited access, a yellow line painted on the floor and a sign that says "stockroom personnel only" are all that are required. What makes these symbolic barriers effective are education and the support of top management. (Thinking back to our previous story, if the CEO had fired the production supervisor on the spot, you could have left the hole in the fence forever, and no one would ever have walked through it.)

In the long run, fortress stockrooms do not serve the interests of the production process. The stockroom is, after all, a service department for production, a place where parts can be stored when not immediately needed on the line or at the shipping dock. As such, it must strike a balance between the requirements of limited access and the need for availability of parts—exactly the same balance that banks have been maintaining for decades. When limited access and scrupulous security become ends in themselves, then the interests of production and sales are not served, and the company is the loser. Stockroom people need to understand that they must initiate and maintain a high level of customer service. They are keepers of a major portion of the company's physical assets, and they need to recognize that their position is vital to operations. Customers of the stockroom, on the other hand, need to understand that limited access is an important tool in assuring that materials are there when they need them and in the right quantities. Thus, limited access and customer service go hand in hand.

Receiving, Inspecting, and Shipping

Limited access is only one principle that a company must support. It must also address the effectiveness of receiving, inspecting, and shipping. Material must be able to move through each of these steps rapidly. It cannot be delayed or unduly held back from production or sales. If material received cannot be put away at the end of each day, the use of *dock receipts* may be necessary. The dock receipt is made from the supplier's packing slip and simply acknowledges, internally, that the material is in-house but has not been formally inspected, counted, or received. For example, if an item has been delivered whose normal stock location is YA12B3, it might be acknowledged with a dock receipt and the material brought into location "Y." It is not placed in its specific location until it has been counted and, if required, inspected. Nonetheless, it is listed on the stock status as an on-hand quantity in location "Y." Anyone looking at the stock status will know that that item has arrived but, because of its location, is not available for use. Once the material has been counted and inspected, a stock-to-stock transfer transaction is made, moving it from "Y" to YA12B3. Any *trailing balance*—that is, a discrepancy between the record and the actual count—would be investigated at this point and either left or purged.

Companies practicing Continuous Improvement methods have streamlined this process further. For example, when material is received at one electronics manufacturer, a receiving attendant uses an expandable conveyor that is pulled directly into the supplier's van. Using a portable bar code device, the attendant acknowledges receipt, creates a bar code label, and puts the label on the side of the box. The bar code receipt updates the transaction file, and the material is then passed along the conveyor directly into the factory. Once in the factory, the material passes another bar code reader that determines its inspection level. If the parts need to be inspected, a gate opens on the conveyor and the material passes down yet another conveyor to an inspection point. "Non-inspect" items move directly to point-of-usage storage areas. The bar code label allows the company to easily and accurately capture movement of the material.

A company does not have to be a Continuous Improvement practitioner to benefit from streamlined receiving and inspection processes. A direct method is to move inspection into the receiving department and make it part of the physical receiving process.

On the other end of the spectrum is a large defense contractor that has a very lengthy quality control inspection and certification process. It uses dock receipts to acknowledge receipt of the parts or material, and follows these with stock-to-stock transfers from the dock to quality control for inspection and certification. A second stock-to-stock transfer transaction is completed by moving the parts or materials from quality control to permanent locations in the stockroom.

Effective Stockroom Layout

Think about your last trip to the supermarket. Chances are it was a clean, well-lighted place with plenty of carts available to make your shopping easy. The different merchandise was arranged in well-marked aisles that were wide enough for maneuvering, yet narrow enough that you could pick from both sides at the same time. Every stock position was clearly labeled with the product's name, price, and even price per ounce. You never had to move a stack of unpacked potato chip cartons to reach a can of tomato sauce. You found no empty lunch bags among the avocados. Everything was carefully arranged and in easy reach. When your selections were completed, checkout was made at a location that quickly and accurately confirmed the identity of each item and in the wink of an eye made an electronic transaction that made a record for you, for the store, and for the inventory system.

The modern stockroom needs many of these same qualities. The layout must allow stockroom personnel easy physical access to the material, and they should not have to move material to get to items. In most cases, you will know whether a company's inventory records are shipshape as soon as you walk into its storeroom. No empty soda cans or candy wrappers are in the bins, and no parts are scattered on the floor. Everything is clean, orderly, and well marked.

Physical Tools

Your supermarket had all the tools that you, as a customer, needed to get in and out quickly with your groceries. Chances are that the supermarket staff had all the hand trucks, carts, forklifts, and so forth, that they needed, too.

Industrial stockrooms also need to consider which physical tools will support accurate and efficient operation. These may include standardized containers, racks, and bins, and material-handling equipment such as forklift trucks, pallet movers, and so forth. These items can be expensive but may be necessary for the attendants to do their jobs well.

The counting scale is another tool that is well worth investigating, especially when large numbers of small, identical parts are involved. The electronic scales available today are more accurate and less expensive than the older-style balance scales. By first determining the average weight of a part through sampling, it then becomes possible to count hundreds of individual parts by means of scales with greater accuracy than can normally be accomplished by physical counts.

Bar coding, as we have just seen, is an extremely useful technology for capturing material movement transactions. By merely waving a light wand, a transaction can be made quickly and accurately. This can eliminate many of the human errors often generated in keying information.

THE PROBLEM OF MULTIPLE STORAGE LOCATIONS

Next to faulty recording of the transactions described earlier, problems associated with multiple stock locations and multiple storage areas for the same part are perhaps the greatest source of inventory record inaccuracy. A shipment of widgets comes to the stockroom by way of receiving, but the storage area for widgets is filled. So where does the shipment go? If it ends up in an overflow area, how will the inventory record keep track of that fact? When widgets are picked to fill a manufacturing order, which widgets should be used first—those in the primary storage area or those in overflow? What if there is more than one storeroom that stocks widgets?

Because these types of questions are so prevalent, we will take a closer look at them, along with some practical solutions. Many companies experience costly losses from multiple location problems. They have the parts—the stock record shows them as "on hand"—but when the time comes to use them, they cannot be found and replacements must be ordered. The system we propose here allows a company to know the precise location of its inventory.

The Power of Piece Count by Multiple Locations

One of the most powerful tools available to the inventory practitioner is the ability to maintain piece count by multiple locations. With this capability, material can be stored in any available location, not solely in a preassigned permanent location. It has been demonstrated that randomly locating inventory provides 40 percent greater space utilization than does the assigning of permanent locations. Multiple location inventory tracking also allows us to maintain inventories that belong to the firm, its customers, and its suppliers without fear of confusion or error. Being able to maintain piece counts by multiple locations also facilitates cycle counting. If 100 parts are stored in each of five locations, a count of 100 in one of those locations will tell us as much about the accuracy of our records and the effectiveness of our methods as the counting of 500 parts in one location.

This capability is made available through a simple software feature that does exactly what its name implies: It allows piece counts by multiple locations. That is, inventory balances for a part physically located in more than one location are maintained on the inventory record for each of those locations. To understand the power of this capability, consider how companies that do not have it might handle certain problems. It is important to remember that we are looking for a process that meets the design criteria of being simple and transparent, and reflects reality.

Consider the following scenario: A stockroom attendant receives into stock three separate shipments of part number 4422: one for 100, a second for 100, and yet another for 1,000. Prior to the first receipt there were zero on hand. With the exception of an overflow area, only 100 of these parts can be stored in any particular location.

Primary Location Only

Using only the primary location, or one location per part, the stock status prior to the first receipt would appear as in Figure 5-1:

Figure 5-1

Part Number	On-hand Quantity	Primary Location
4422	0	YA11A1

Upon receipt of the first 100 pieces, put in the primary location, the record appears as in Figure 5-2.

Figure 5-2

Part Number	On-hand Quantity	Primary Location
4422	100	YA11A1

So far, so good. The transaction is simple and transparent: 100 pieces are received and put into location YA11A1, just as the record reflects. It also passes the tough test of representing reality. That is, there are 100 pieces of 4422 in location YA11A1.

Problems develop, however, when the second receipt is processed. Because the primary location—YA11A1—is filled to capacity with the first 100, the stock attendant has to search for a second location. An empty location is found at YB22B2, and the second 100 is located there. The record now appears as in Figure 5-3.

Figure 5-3

Part Number	On-hand Quantity	Primary Location
4422	200	YA11A1

This second receipt causes the *primary-location-only method* to flunk two critical design criteria. First, the simplicity test is strained. Without first knowing that location YA11A1 can hold only 100 pieces, the stock attendant would seek that location to consolidate inventory because it is listed as the primary location. Finding it full, the attendant then finds an alternate location in YB22B2. The record says, however, that there are 200 pieces in YA11A1. It thus fails the reality criterion. To satisfy this, a paper chain consisting of a note attached to the parts in the primary location is created that tells other stock attendants that more 4422s can be found in location YB22B2.

> To: Dave and Archie
> Ran out of space in this bin. 100 more 4422s in YB22B2.
>
>   Dale

The next day 1,000 pieces are received, and the record reflects 1,200 pieces in YA11A1. When the attendant tries to store them, YA11A1 is full, but Dale's paper chain reflects the second location, YB22B2. The stock attendant tries to consolidate these additional 1,000 there. That location is also full, but she finds an open overflow location at YC33C3 and stores the 1,000 there. The paper chain is then updated to reflect the new location. Figure 5-4 shows the new stock status report.

Figure 5-4

Part Number	On-hand Quantity	Primary Location
4422	1,200	YA11A1

The next day a new attendant is put on the job. He is told to pick 1,200 of part number 4422 from location YA11A1. He finds YA11A1 and scoops up all the parts along with the attached paper chain. As he passes data entry, he hands over the issue transaction. As he heads out to the factory floor, the paper chain floats off and is lost forever. The data entry person makes the inventory transaction, issuing 1,200, and the inventory record reflects that there are now zero of part number 4422 in stock.

A few hours later, the stockroom phone rings. It's the production supervisor, who wants to know the whereabouts of 1,100 of part number 4422. There are supposed to be 1,200 at the assembly line right now, but he has only 100. The new attendant is asked about it and swears that all were issued because the location is now empty.

Thus begins the process of finding the missing parts, sometimes known as "walking the racks." Like children on an Easter egg hunt, stockroom staff begin the truly ridiculous process of combing the aisles and bins for the missing 4422s.

A Better and Recommended Way

A simpler and much more effective approach is to list these parts by multiple locations. Piece count by multiple locations is a software architecture issue, and software either has the capability or it does not. Some companies already have this capability in their software but do not use it. Programming it into existing software is relatively easy if the right approach is used.

Figure 5-5 illustrates a stock status (on-hand balance report) using piece counts by multiple locations for part 4422. This is the recommended practice.

A software variation may cite the multiple locations for part number 4422 and the total on-hand quantity but not the *specific quantity* stored in each. This variation is obviously inferior to what we have in Figure 5-5, where we know both how much is stored and where it is stored.

The advantages of piece count by multiple locations are far greater than might be expected for such a simple technique. The most obvious and important of these is that parts can be located quickly and easily. Piece count by multiple locations also meets the critical design criteria of being simple, transparent, and representative of reality. It also allows

Figure 5-5

Part Number	On-hand Quantity	Location
4422	100	YA11A1
	100	YB22B2
	1,000	YC33C3
TOTAL	1,200	

a company to maintain multiple locations and an overflow area without fear of confusion. Companies will often purchase parts in large quantities, particularly items such as fasteners and nuts and bolts. It is often necessary to have overflow areas so that large purchase quantities don't impede the efficiency of the stockroom. These overflow areas are listed in the multiple location field as distinct locations.

Storage locations outside the storeroom proper can also be tracked with the multiple location feature. These may include the following:

- Point-of-use storage areas

- Multiple warehouses or stockrooms that store the same parts

- Receiving areas

- Inspection areas

- Any department or facility

ISSUING PARTS FROM MULTIPLE LOCATIONS

The next time you are in the supermarket, observe the way in which perishable items such as milk are stored in the refrigerator cases. Most stores today use back-loading refrigerators. The customer opens the front door and usually takes a milk carton from the front row. As these are taken, the grocer adds new, fresher cartons in the back. The grocer has set up a particular "issuing logic"—in this case, the classic first-in, first-out (FIFO) arrangement—to assure that neither he nor the customer ends up with spoiled milk.

Issuing from Location of Largest Quantity

Manufacturers with multiple inventory locations need to consider issuing logic—a form of decision rule—for their inventory. Inventory rotation or contract requirements are two possible premises for issuing by
location, but there are others. To illustrate this, let's look at the on-hand
balances for part number 4422 as in Figure 5-6.

Figure 5-6

Part Number	On-hand Quantity	Primary Location
4422	100	YA11A1
	100	YB22B2
	1,000	YC33C3
TOTAL	1,200	

If an issue requires a quantity of 200, they could logically be picked
from the 1,000 in location YC33C3. This would be the most efficient for
the stock attendants because they would have to go to only one stock
location to complete the transaction. The issue logic would then be
"issue first from the location with the largest on-hand quantity." However, this issue logic is efficient for only a short period of time. The
practice eventually creates many locations with small quantities in each.
When this is done with all parts throughout a stockroom or warehouse,
it causes the facility to become full of partially filled locations. A much
better practice is to issue from the location with the smallest quantities
first—in this example, 100 each from locations YA11A1 and YB22B2.
This automatically purges these two locations and leaves a single location, YC33C3, with 1,000 pieces.

The efficiency of this practice is then realized in the activities of
issuing and the putting away of parts that follow. A stockroom manager
should give considerable thought to this example before issuing always
from the location with the largest on-hand quantity.

As stated earlier, random locations offer greater storage density. If
permanent locations are utilized for certain parts, however, the issuing

logic should recognize this requirement and always specify those locations for issuing.

Rotating Inventory

Rotating inventory on a first-in, first-out (FIFO) basis is, as we have seen, a way to reduce losses due to aging and also encourage the simultaneous use of dated components. The latter situation is of particular importance for manufacturers who use components such as engines. It is difficult to explain to a customer why her 1992 vehicle has a 1990 engine (the serial number tells the story, even though there may be no physical or performance difference between engines made in either year).

The easiest way to ensure inventory rotation is to carry a date field on the stock status report by location. The date that the parts are put into their specific location is automatically recorded in this field. See Figure 5-7. The issuing logic would then be "first in, first out."

Figure 5-7

Part Number	On-hand Quantity	Location	Received Date
4422	100	YA11A1	2/2/93
	100	YB22B2	3/3/93
	1,000	YC33C3	6/6/93
TOTAL	1,200		

Should 50 pieces of part number 4422 be required, the issuing logic should specify location YA11A1 because this contains the oldest inventory. Note that the "Received Date" specifies when the part was last put into this location. This is updated if more inventory is added to an existing location and thus precludes the practice of consolidating inventory into existing locations.

Lot/Batch and Contract Control

Much like the need for inventory rotation, some companies are required to maintain lot or batch control numbers; that is, a steel mill might roll several tons of steel plate from a single pour. All of the plate rolled from this pour should be assigned a lot number. The logic behind this is that should a component fabricated from the steel plate experience failure due to the chemistry of the steel, all components made from plate of the same lot would be suspect. Batch numbers are utilized in chemical, pharmaceutical, and food processing industries for similar reasons. Lot/batch control is often an element of quality assurance programs. Other firms are under some form of contractual obligation to use parts from specified lots or batches. These obligations may be the result of government requirements or the requirements of a customer's contract. In these situations, it is just as important to know what lot, batch, or contract the inventory belongs to as it is to properly issue and track its use.

These situations can be successfully addressed with an approach analogous to the "received date" method used with rotating inventory. In these cases, the extra data field is not used to retain the received date but the batch or contract number (or a derivative thereof). In some contract control situations, the customer or regulatory agency may give a company permission to physically commingle pieces.[1] Rarely, if ever, will a company be able to commingle pieces when lot control is being tracked.

The stock status report for a lot or contract control part might appear as in Figure 5-8.

Figure 5-8

Part Number	On-hand Quantity	Location	Lot/Contract Control
4422	100	YA11A1	AF-004
	100	YB22B2	NV-123
	1,000	YC33C3	AR-878
TOTAL	1,200		

---

[1] Physically commingling in this context means mixing the parts themselves. If two bags of parts are stored in the same location but remain separated and identified by bag, they are not considered physically commingled. If the contents of both bags are emptied into another, larger container, they are commingled.

The lot/contract number is assigned to the parts either when they are ordered or when they are received. The number is noted on the receiving documents and is physically attached to the pieces involved. It is also reported, entered, and retained when the parts are put into stock. The stock status simply stores the lot, batch, or contract number. Tracing or tracking these numbers would be done through the transaction history file. It requires that the lot number be recorded when the parts are issued. Then it must be entered and retained as part of the transaction representing the issue event.

When the establishment of ownership is a requirement, as when the customer owns the parts and/or materials stored in the manufacturer's storeroom, the contract number makes this explicit. For example, in Figure 5-8, AF-004 means "Air Force," thus committing the part to a specific Air Force contract.

Proper use of the pieces offers a bigger challenge. In Figure 5-8, only the pieces in location YA11A1 can be used on contract AF-004, and those in location YB22B2 on contract NV-123. Therefore, it is an absolute requirement that those parts be issued for those contracts only. To facilitate this, the issuing program logic needs to capture a contract number; then only the parts associated with that number can be specified for issuing. Using pieces from other contracts should be done only with approval from the regulatory agencies involved.

The Issuing Logic of Standard Software
We have yet to see issuing logic in standard software systems that completely meets the needs of any manufacturing company. This area tends to be one in which the software needs to be customized to some degree.

One requirement of software is certain, however: It should allow the user to employ each and every issuing logic needed for each and every part number. A single field in the part master file can be used to accommodate this. The software should have the capability for the issuing logic to be different for different components. For example, suppose our part master file has components 1000, 2000, and 3000. Part number 1000 is always issued from the location with the lowest on-hand quantity, while P/N 2000's logic is FIFO, and P/N 3000 will always be controlled by a contract number. All of this can be accomplished with a one-position data field in the item master file:

P/N	On Hand	Location	Contract	Date In	Issue Logic
1000	25	YA12B3		02-02-02	A
	15	YB04C1		03-03-92	A
Total	40				
2000	55	YE05A3		04-04-92	B
	5	YR07D2		05-05-92	B
Total	60				
3000	75	YB09C4	NV-123	07-07-92	C

Key: A = Issue from lowest on-hand inventory
 B = Issue from oldest inventory first
 C = Issue by contract number

PRACTICAL ISSUING CONSIDERATIONS

The modern workplace presents many more special inventory situations than can be anticipated and explained in any book. The practitioner in these cases is advised to think of creative solutions that pass the fundamental tests of simplicity, transparency, and reality.

A little foresight in the design of issuing logic can help solve some of these special inventory situations. One such case involved a low-volume forklift manufacturer that issued parts for a week's production all at one time. Naturally, this created problems on the factory floor. Engines, transmissions, drive axles, and hoods were large and difficult to hold in weekly quantities in the assembly area. Additionally, the final product had a high option orientation, and different engine transmissions, hoods, and valve types were required. That meant a lot of different parts out on the floor. The final assembly supervisor sequenced the different trucks and their options as best fit the customers' needs and his own capacity. Unfortunately, there were so many parts piled up in the assembly area that the work flow was severely impaired.

After much thought, it was decided to give the assembly supervisor *issue tickets* instead of the parts they represented. These issue tickets were printed in multiples of ones, or in a logical multiple of the suppliers' packaging, or a convenient material-handling quantity. Engines were 1 per issue ticket, as were transmissions and drive axles. Hoods were in multiples of 3 because that was how they were bundled. Radiators were in multiples of 5 and batteries in multiples of 12. These latter 2 items were easily damaged, and it was desirable not to unpack them prior to their use in assembly.

The issue tickets were specially coded so they could be sorted from the rest and given to the final assembly supervisor, like uncashed cashier's checks. When presented to the stockroom, they could be exchanged for the parts they represented. It became standard operating practice for the final assembly supervisor to plan the next day's assembly sequence and determine which major components he would like in his area the following morning. He would then sort those issue tickets from his deck and present them to the stockroom. His parts would then be issued and delivered to his area for the next morning's assembly activities. Inventory movement transactions were also captured from the issue tickets.

Rejected Parts

Inventory items are periodically rejected for any number of reasons, but rejections cannot just be tossed in trash cans or automatically returned to suppliers without some form of accounting to the inventory record system. Whenever material is rejected, someone must determine its final disposition, and a proper accounting of that disposition must be made. These tasks are simplified by the creation of a separate location called the Material Review Board (MRB) and a requirement that rejected material awaiting disposition be physically placed in it. To the inventory records, the MRB is just another location and is tracked accordingly. Once disposition has been determined, the material should be immediately scrapped, issued to a rework order, or moved to a "return to supplier" location, and the appropriate transaction recorded.

Company policy should limit the time that material can reside in the

MRB to 48 hours; otherwise, it will become a growing clutter of inventory.

Borrowed Parts

The sales manager for the midwest district was having all of his reps in the office for a summer product training session. He planned to have samples of each of the company's new products on hand to point out important new features. Of course, he did not request the items through inventory; he figured that he would just stop at the warehouse that morning and pick up what he needed.

The warehouse had just opened as he arrived. "Where's Fred?" he asked the warehouse supervisor's assistant in the front office.

"He's in the lunch room."

"Okay," said the sales manager as he went past the assistant. But instead of going to see Fred, he headed directly toward the finished goods shelves, where he found the 12 parts he needed, stuffed them into his attaché case, and went back through the office.

"See ya!" he shouted to the assistant.

Later that morning, stock pickers came up short on some parts listed in a rush order to an important customer. No one knew why they were short.

Borrowing stock items goes on all the time and normally serves an important business function. Engineering, sales, service, and advertising personnel often need samples of finished goods or parts for a short period of time to carry on their work. That inventory belongs to the stockroom, however, unless those particular departments actually "buy" it through their departmental account numbers. Stockroom personnel need to know where it is and be accountable for it. If the borrower is established as a stocking location, then borrowed inventory can be transferred and tracked without damage to the integrity of the inventory records. For example, a stock-to-stock transfer to "ENGR BEV" will result in a new stock location reflecting that Engineer Beverly has a specified part.[2]

---

[2] If the issuing logic specifies issuing from the location with the smallest quantity first, it will remind the stock attendants of Engineer Beverly's "borrowed" part every time a pick is made.

"In-transit" Items

A man returned home from a business trip unexpectedly a day early, only to find his wife entertaining another man. "Why are you here?" the angry husband demanded of the stranger.

"Everybody has to be somewhere" was the reply.

Parts, too, have to be "somewhere" at all times, and this poses a challenge to inventory systems when company stock locations are separated by great distances. Here again, the ability to record multiple locations provides a solution.

If a company stockroom "S" is located in Seattle and stockroom "P" is on the outskirts of Portland, Oregon, a simple stock-to-stock transfer between these two locations may not be desirable. The moment stockroom "S" performs the stock-to-stock transfer to stockroom "P," the material is subtracted from the balance of stockroom "S" while upgrading the balance in stockroom "P." A problem can arise when someone wants to know why the material isn't in stockroom "P" when it's still sitting on the pallet in stockroom "S" waiting to be moved. In this circumstance, creation of an "in-transit" stocking location solves the problem. The locator system shows that the material is in transit and is not in one stockroom or the other. When the material is received by the second stockroom, a stock-to-stock transfer is completed, from "in transit" to stockroom "P." Again, this procedure makes the record-keeping process a mirror of reality.

LOCATING SYSTEMS

Once the ability to track stock parts by location—and multiple locations—is developed, it is important to give some thought to a system that specifies a unique storage area for each part. In an ideal world, one with neither space nor economic constraints, every part would have its own designated place. But the practical world makes such a tidy system less than ideal.

Location by Part Number

Some manufacturers and distributors with small parts use a part number sequence. For example, part 1001 is in the first location; part 1002 is in the second location; part 1003 is in the third location. Although this is straightforward and seems initially to eliminate the need for a separate locating system, it has a number of practical flaws. This becomes evident when part numbers not initially stocked are added or when the quantities of the original parts are increased.

To illustrate, imagine a city in which citizens live in alphabetically arranged houses, as determined by their last names. The Ables might be in the first house on the first street, the Adamses in the second house on the same street, followed by the Bakers and the Browns. The Zaltmans would probably live in the last occupied house on the last street. With such an arrangement, house addresses would not be required. Each family would simply put its surname on the front door. Street names would be unnecessary; each street would be labeled with the first and last family names found on that street—like a page in a dictionary. Those looking for the Joneses would walk down the street and check the surnames. If the surname on the house they were standing in front of was Baker, they would keep walking through the alphabet. If they saw Monlux on the house, they would then walk in the opposite direction. This would be a simple system. However, if a new family named the Aarons were to move into town, they would have to move into the Ables' house. The Ables would have to move next door, displacing the Bakers, and so on throughout the city. In essence, every family would be required to move one house. This would be a big headache for everyone except the moving and title companies, for whom the system would be a license to make money.

Similarly, a space problem might develop if the Bergers had triplets and their in-laws moved in with them at the same time. The city locating system would not allow them to move to a larger house. Likewise, if the Smiths did not like living between the Slaters and the Stulls, they would be out of luck because the alphabetical household system would prevent them from relocating.

The ridiculous constraints this system places on people are similar to the problems a stockroom encounters when parts are located in part number sequence. When a new part is introduced, all those with a higher number must be moved to allow space. The same thing may happen if a large quantity of a part is received and its present location is not adequate to handle it. Finally, stock attendants may want to store many parts close to one another for issuing ease or because of special requirements, and this would take them out of part number sequence.

These problems of stocking parts in part number sequence are often ingeniously overcome or tolerated in the stockroom. People do make it work. However, the high cost of this approach is never fully recognized by anyone other than the people who must work with it day after day. A far better approach is to use a locating system that is not tied to part numbers.

The Independent Locating System

A common solution to the problem described above is to have a locating system that is independent of the part numbering system. Each aisle, rack, bin, and/or opening has its own address, just as every city lot—whether it has a building on it or not—has a street address. When parts are placed in a location, that address is noted. This allows parts to be stored in locations of choice, to include multiple locations. It is recommended in most situations that the system relating part numbers, quantities, and locations be designed to allow more than one part number in a location. A location should not be limited to one specific part number; in other words, P/N 1000 and P/N 2525 can both be located in YA06B4. Functional software does not restrict locations and part numbers to one for one.

Addresses

One of the most common methods of assigning addresses to stockroom locations is to give a name to a row of racks or bins; then a name to each vertical rack opening or stack of bins within the row; and finally to the shelves themselves. Thus, the address A-03-B would be the second shelf (B) in the third rack (03) in row "A." The next row of racks would be "B," and the address B-03-B would be exactly across the aisle from A-03-B (if rack rows A and B shared the same aisle).

While this approach has merit, a superior addressing system is one that names the aisles instead of the rack rows. This system mirrors an effective addressing system with which everyone is already familiar: the city street address. Addresses in cities do not call all the houses on one side of a street by one name and the houses on the other side a different name. The street bears the name and the houses on either side are designated with odd or even numbers. Thus, if we have location Y-A-03-B2, as in Figure 5-9, the Y identifies the particular stockroom, A the aisle, 03 the rack, B the shelf, and 2 the opening on that shelf. These addresses are analogous to city, street, building, floor, and apartment. The last figure of the stockroom address always designates the smallest locational element (an opening); the first always designates the largest (the particular stockroom). This system has proven most effective.

Figure 5-9   Stockroom Addressing

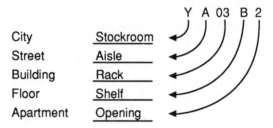

City	Stockroom
Street	Aisle
Building	Rack
Floor	Shelf
Apartment	Opening

A typical location again might be A-03-B. This identifies the second shelf (B) in the second rack (03) on the left-hand side of aisle A. Note that all the right-hand-side openings are even and would appear in the following sequence: 02, 04, 06, 08. The rack openings exactly opposite those, on the left-hand side of the aisle, would be numbered 01, 03, 05, 07.

The advantages of this addressing system are twofold: First, it is easy to learn because people learned to use this system as children and have been using it ever since. Second, it allows a stock attendant to pick all the parts in a particular aisle, both sides, in one pass if the picking document is listed in address sequence.

More than one stockroom can be accommodated in this system by simply adding a preface letter to the aisle, rack, or shelf: Y-A-03-B; the specific opening within the shelf can be accommodated with a suffix number: Y-A-03-B-2 (stockroom-aisle-rack-shelf-opening). Again, this is analogous to the addressing system used by the U. S. Postal Service: city-street-address-floor-apartment. Since the hyphens between the characters become bothersome in data entry, they are often dropped, leaving YA03B2. It is important to note that when the shelves are named, they should be named from the floor up. The lowermost shelf is A, the next shelf up B, and so on. This is preferable to starting at the top and labeling downward because the expansion of storage is never downward.

Whenever an independent addressing system is used, it is wise to label vacant locations even if no storage racks or bins are presently in those locations. This is analogous to providing an address for vacant lots in a city. If a house is built on it, the house uses the lot address, and none of the houses farther down the street need to be readdressed.

Work-in-Process Areas

Work-in-process areas are usually labeled by work centers and/or column grids. When the work center convention is used, each work center (a machine, group of machines, and/or workstation) is assigned an identification of some type: PC001, W/C 017, MACH 123, or STA 222 (PC = Piston Center, W/C = Work Center, MACH = Machine, and STA = Station). Knowing the physical locations of these work centers is a matter of memorization, like knowing where the states of Oregon, Vermont, and New York are located on a map. There is no particular rhyme or reason to these locations; they are merely something we need to memorize. Although this system leaves much to be desired in terms of logic, it works fairly well if the work-in-process area is relatively small and the plant is not in a constant state of being reconfigured.

The column grid system, by contrast, is more logical and lends itself more easily to the Continuous Improvement practitioner who does not have a stockroom and is storing parts and material at the point of use. This method assigns names to the intersections of the areas between the columns in the plant. A column (support structure) layout is drawn, and the horizontal areas are assigned a numerical designator while the vertical areas are assigned an alphabetical designator (see Figure 5-10). Anyone familiar with city maps will recognize this system of grid cells. Thus, in Figure 5-10, location A-04 is in the extreme upper right address area. Here again, having the ability to account for pieces by multiple locations turns these designations into accountable inventory locations.

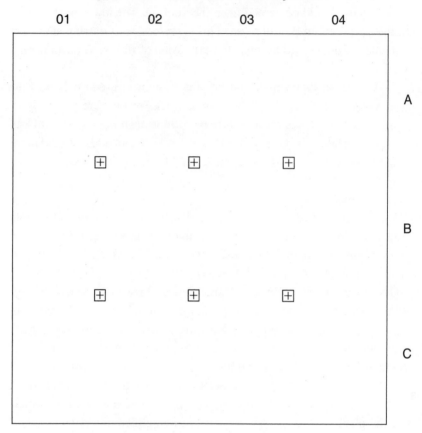

Figure 5-10   The Column Grid System

REPORTS AND SCREENS

As we have seen, the ability to create multiple locations, identify them by means of a logical "street" address system, and issue from any of them gives a firm tremendous power to manage its inventory. But to maintain accurate records for that system, four basic reports/screens are required:

1. Stock status by part number (Figure 5-11, page 83)

2. Stock status by location (Figure 5-12, page 84)

Figure 5-11   Stock Status by Part Number

                                                (1.)
                                           12/11/XX

(2.) PART#	(3.) DESCRIPTION	(4.) STK LOC	(5.) STK OH	(6.) UM	(7.) CC DATE	(8.) LAST TRANS	(9.) TOL
71639	BOOSTER	YN 37B2	22	EA	00/00/00	12/09/XX	0%
71640	CYLINDER	RG 06B2	174		10/09/XX	12/04/XX	0%
		YB 50E3	25		12/05/XX	12/04/XX	0%
		YC 12D1	11		11/11/XX	12/10/XX	0%
			210	EA			
72692	TUBE	RA 05A1	20	FT	08/19/XX	11/08/XX	5%
73154	BAL STUD	YD 11B1 (14.)	0	EA	10/23/XX	12/10/XX	2%
73155	SWITCH	(10.) ASSY 17 Y	14		12/05/XX	12/02/XX	5%
			600		00/00/00	12/10/XX	5%
		(11.) YE 14A2	70		10/14/XX	12/06/XX	5%
			684	EA			
73156	HUB	(12.) ENGR BEV	1		00/00/00	04/04/XX	2%
		MRB	400		00/00/00	12/06/XX	2%
		(13.) RC 13C2	90		12/01/XX	12/07/XX	2%
			491	EA			

- -

1. Report Date

2. Part Number (Sort Sequence)

3. Part Description

4. Stock Location

5. Stock on Hand in Specific Location

6. Unit of Measure
   (Print by Total on Hand)

7. Last Cycle Count Date
   at Specific Location

8. Last Transaction Date
   in Specific Location

9. Cycle Counting Tolerance

10. Point of Use Location

11. Receiving Area of Stockroom "Y"

12. Engineer Borrowed

13. Material Review Board

14. Zero on Hand Balances Retained
    for Cycle Counting

3. Inventory transaction history by part number (Figure 5-13, page 85), which details all the events that have affected that particular part number in a specified number of prior weeks or months. Few software packages include this report. They often provide the ability to see *all* the transactions that take place during any given

Figure 5-12   Stock Status by Location

①.

12/11/XX

②. PART#	③. DESCRIPTION	④. STK LOC	⑤. STK OH	⑥. UM	⑦. CC DATE	⑧. LAST TRANS	⑨. TOL
89043	PIN	YC 12C1	600	EA	00/00/00	12/08/XX	2%
89043	PIN	YC 12C2	600	EA	00/00/00	12/08/XX	2%
14263	STARTER	YC 12C3	1	EA	12/05/XX	11/14/XX	0%
62999	ALTERNATOR	YC 12C3	2	EA	12/05/XX	10/16/XX	0%
71640	CYLINDER	YC 12D1	11	EA	11/11/XX	12/10/XX	0%
15239	POWER SUPP	YC 12D2	10	EA	12/05/XX	12/03/XX	0%
72642	HOSE	YC 13A1	50	FT	12/05/XX	11/16/XX	5%
59899	BRACKET	YC 13A2	17	EA	12/05/XX	10/21/XX	2%
40017	HOSE	YC 13A3	100	FT	12/05/XX	11/22/XX	5%

- -

1. Report Date
2. Part Number
3. Part Description
4. Stock Location (Stock Sequence)
5. Stock on Hand in Specific Location

6. Unit of Measure
7. Last Cycle Count Date
   at Specific Location
8. Last Transaction Date in
   Specific Location
9. Cycle Counting Tolerance

day, but these are not all transactions affecting a specific part number over time. The importance of the transaction history report will become clearer when we discuss cycle counting in Chapter 7.

4. Open order listing (Figure 5-14, page 86) showing what supply orders are owed the company or are work-in-process

Figure 5-13 Transaction History

(1.) PART NUMBER: 71640	(2.) DESC: CYCLINDER	(3.) MAKE/BUY: BUY	(4.) PLANNER:7	(5.) BUYER:A

(6.) PROC DATE	(7.) TRANS	(8.) TRANS/DATE	(9.) QUANTITY	(10.) ORDER/ACCT	(11.) FROM LOC	(12.) TO LOC	(13.) CLK
12/11/XX	ISS	12/10/XX	6	J12362	YC 12D1		37
12/11/XX	ISS	12/10/XX	5	J12361	YC 12D1		37
12/06/XX	CC	12/05/XX	25		YB 50E3		49
12/05/XX	STS	12/04/XX	25		RG 06B2	YB 50E3	37
11/30/XX	ISS	11/29/XX	26	DM6234	MRB		37
11/12/XX	CC	11/11/XX	22		YC 12D1		49
11/07/XX	RTS	11/06/XX	22	J11432		YC 12D1	37
10/10/XX	CC	10/09/XX	199		RG 06B2		49
09/19/XX	STS	09/18/XX	199		R	RG 06B2	07
09/19/XX	STS	09/18/XX	26	R92431	R	MRB	52
09/18/XX	REC	09/17/XX	225	P24639		R	22

TRANSACTION KEY:

REC = Receipt

ISS = Issue

STS = Stock-to-Stock Transfer

RTS = Return to Stock

SCR = Scrap

CC = Cycle Count

SA = Stock Adjustment

1. Part Number
2. Part Description
3. Make or Buy Code
4. Planner Code
5. Buyer Code
6. Date Transaction Processed
7. Transaction Type (see Key)
8. Date of Transaction
9. Quantity of This Transaction
10. Authorization or Order Number
11. Issued from Location
12. Issued to Location
13. Employee or Clock Number

These figures are, of course, for illustration purposes only. Each company must design these reports to fit its specific requirements, and their design must mirror exactly what is happening with the company's inventory.

It is extremely important that these reports be available either in hard copy or on a computer terminal and that they are updated *at least* daily

Figure 5-14   Open Order Listing

(1.)

12/11/xx

(2.)   (3.)   (4.)   (5.)   (6.) (7.) (8.) (9.) (10.)

			QUANTITY						
PART #	ORDER #	DESC	ORIG	BAL	U/M	DUE	BYR	PLNR	SUPPLIER
14263	P45722	STARTER	100	100	ea	4/1/xx	D	05	05316
15239	P45806	POWER SUP	50	50	ea	1/8/xx	D	02	00782
40017	P47085	HOSE	200	200	ft	1/5/xx	B	02	01166
59899	M02907	BRACKET	10	10	ea	2/1/xx	M	02	00001
62999	P45723	ALTERNATOR	100	100	ea	4/1/xx	D	05	05316
71639	P45771	BOOSTER	60	60	ea	2/1/xx	C	03	01994
71640	P46007	CYLINDER	225	35	ea	1/2/xx	C	03	01994
73156	M03002	HUB	300	300	ea	3/1/xx	M	04	00001

1. Report Date

2. Part Number (Default Sort Sequence)

3. Order Number (Optional Sort Sequence)

4. Description

5. Original Quality on Order and Current Balance on Order

6. Unit of Measure

7. Acknowledged Delivery Date (Optional Sort Sequence)

8. Buyer Code (Optional Sort Sequence)

9. Planner Code (Optional Sort Sequence)

10. Supplier Code (Optional Sort Sequence)

Note: The authors believe it is acceptable to list all open orders on a single report – as shown here– or separate them for purchased and manufactured parts. In either case, the ability to sort by selected field can be very useful.

and always by the beginning of each working day. This means that *all* transactions from the previous day, including second and third shifts, must be processed and reflected on the balances of each morning's reports. The inventory balances need to be up to date and accurate so that planners, schedulers, and buyers can make informed supply/

withdrawals are updated daily so that tellers, loan officers, and managers can make decisions with the most up-to-date balances.

ISSUE LISTS AND ISSUE DECKS

Once the reports have been designed, attention must be turned to the design of the *issuing documents*, which are the physical documents that communicate specifically how much of what needs to be issued to where. When parts are to be issued, particularly from a stockroom where many different parts are stored, it is often necessary to generate a document that specifies part number, quantity, and location. These documents are often called "issue/pick lists" or "issue/pick decks." (The term "parts list" is often incorrectly used in reference to this document.) Issue lists and issue decks differ only in the form in which they are presented. An *issue list* is normally one document that lists all the parts to be issued, while an *issue deck* is a number of documents, often cards, each listing one part number and location.

The choice of using either issue lists or issue decks should be made by those doing the issuing. When the number of parts to be issued is small, 5 to 10 per order, it makes little difference which method is used. However, when the number is large, more than 30 parts, the advantages and disadvantages of lists versus decks become more obvious.

The issue list is typically favored by those who enter the transactions rather than the person who has to physically pick the parts. The list is favored since one transaction can be used to represent the activity performed on the entire list of part numbers. Thus, one entry covers all the parts on the list. Stock attendants, on the other hand, must then either carry a long list with them as they pick the parts or divide the list among them by physically cutting the document into pieces.

Although a list is handy for transacting the issuing activities, it can present problems when it arrives near the end of a day or shift. In this situation, the list may get only partially issued. Then, to ensure a clean data cutoff, those parts that have actually been issued (or those parts not yet issued) must be individually entered. (This would require the design of a "do not transact" list or an "only those noted transact" list or possibly an "except for those noted" list.) Because of this data entry load, many companies don't start picking a list unless sufficient time remains in the day or work shift to finish the list in its entirety. Here, issuing decks have the advantage of being easily divided and distributed to many stock attendants who can pick the same order simultaneously. The documents are normally printed on cards or labels small enough to be handled easily. Frequently, a portion of the issuing deck document is attached to the parts themselves for identification purposes. Historically, punched cards were used for this purpose. They were perforated, and a small portion of the card was attached to the issued parts. The remaining portion was used to enter the transaction. With the advent of bar codes, however, many companies began to attach the entire issue deck document, which includes a bar code, to the part as an identification label and then "wand it" to record the transaction.

One of the best ways to avoid the conflict between issue lists and issue decks is to have the issue list divided into pages and provide an electronic facsimile of it on the data entry terminal screen. A lengthy issue list can then be separated and distributed by pages to several stock attendants. As they issue the parts, they can note any deviations in actual locations and/or quantities. When a page is completed, the data entry person simply brings up the page on the terminal representing the original issue page. That screen is then changed to represent the actual issues and is transacted as an entire page.

FINAL PREPARATION: EDUCATION, TRAINING, AND ASSIGNMENT OF RESPONSIBILITY

Once a company has designed its inventory process, policies, and procedures, it is ready to begin the final step in the first phase of the plan to achieve inventory record accuracy. That step has three parts:

1. The education of all personnel who in any way interface with the inventory system. A good case can be made that education should be addressed at the very beginning of the design and preparation phase, particularly for those individuals assigned to the design

team. They need to understand the importance of record accuracy to the larger goals of the firm.

2. Training of those individuals who will be directly involved in using and maintaining the newly designed inventory records system

3. The assignment of responsibility for inventory record accuracy to specific individuals

The importance of this final step cannot be overemphasized. No matter how well crafted the inventory process may be, it will not deliver 95 percent or better accuracy if it is placed in the hands of people who are ill-trained to use it. It would be like putting the finest, most accurate target pistol into the hands of someone who has not learned how to sight and shoot. The person will still miss the target by a wide margin.

Education

Everyone who comes into contact with the inventory system must understand why accurate inventory records are needed. This includes top management, middle management, buyers, planners, schedulers, engineering, marketing, sales, and labor. All need to know how and where these records will be used, and how their use requires a different set of employee behaviors. Our earlier example of the sales manager who blithely walked off with a dozen inventory items speaks to this point.

Education has two critically important objectives: fact transfer and behavior change. Fact transfer, in this instance, takes place when people learn the use and mechanics of inventory record accuracy. Fact transfer occurs, for example, when floor supervisors learn the inventory records must be maintained to a minimum of 95 percent accuracy if the MRP or Continuous Improvement program hopes to succeed. Behavior change occurs when people appreciate the need to do their jobs differently—in this case, in ways that allow the newly designed inventory record system to function as intended. Most managers, planners, buyers, floor supervisors, and workers already understand how MRP and CI can make their firms more effective and competitive and their own jobs easier. Behavior change occurs when these same people recognize that having a minimum of 95 percent inventory record accuracy is the foundation for those important systems and that the tangible benefits are fewer shortages and stock-outs, less down time, and less time wasted on physically checking stockroom balances.[3]

Training

A company need not hire new people to operate and maintain its newly designed inventory record system. Chances are that current stockroom personnel can handle the new tools effectively—but only if adequate training is provided.

Anyone involved in this training process should know that stockroom personnel need to know more than simply *how* to do things; they need to understand *why*, as well. Answering the "why" question is done through the educational process described earlier. Answering the "how" question is accomplished through a careful explanation of policies and procedures, including the proper execution of transactions, location changes, and so forth.

A good place to begin the training process is with the flowchart (as described in Chapter 4) that represents the movement of parts and materials throughout the facility. The next step is to decide which transactions are necessary to capture those movements and at which points the company wants to capture them. Then the transactions themselves need to be designed, stating what kind of transactions they are and all the pertinent information. Finally, procedures must be written that clearly describe all the steps involved in the process, including how to fill out or key in transactions.

We recommend a training process that incorporates the use of a Caramate audio/slide player. This viewing device is a cube of about 18 inches on a side that combines a carousel slide projector and an audiocassette tape player. It allows a company to graphically illustrate what it wants its people to do. The advantages of a Caramate over other forms of training aids are as follows:

---

[3] A complete narrative on the subject of educating for behavior change can be found in Thomas F. Wallace, *MRP II: Making It Happen* (Essex Junction, VT: Oliver Wight Limited Publications, Inc., 1985), p. 81.

- It is inexpensive.

- It is easy to revise its audio tapes and 35mm slides.

- A professional presentation can be produced with very little training or experience.

- The message is consistent.

- It travels well and is simple to set up and use.

All the different forms and transactions that will have to be filled out in the stockroom can be photographed against a felt backdrop, one field or block at a time. These can be synchronized with a cassette voice track that describes what needs to be placed in each of the fields. Each field and its accompanying description can then be indexed for ease and speed of handling. Once this recording and slide-preparation task has been done, the company will have a complete audiovisual presentation tool for training its personnel on how to fill out each of its forms and transactions. It can be sent to geographically separated stockrooms and used repeatedly for retraining or to train new personnel.

Assignment of Responsibility
Once all the necessary people have been educated, the next step is to assign responsibilities for action and results. Long experience with managing people and processes has indicated that if a satisfactory outcome is to be achieved, someone must have both the responsibility for assuring that outcome and the resources and authority necessary to make it happen. As Harry Truman said of his office, "The buck stops here."

Theoretically, President Truman was assigned the ultimate responsibility for everything the U.S. government did or failed to do. As a practical matter, a better result is accomplished when responsibility for an activity is assigned at the lowest possible level—that is, as close to the action as possible. In the case of designing, implementing, and maintaining an accurate inventory record system, the CEO or general manager has the ultimate responsibility, but the person normally assigned responsibility is the stockroom manager. The reason is simple: The stockroom manager will be the person accountable for record accuracy on an ongoing basis. Given the education, the support, and the tools, the stockroom manager can then be held responsible for getting the job done. We will take a closer look at the responsibilities and performance evaluation of the stockroom manager in Chapter 9.

Chapter 6

Phase II: Establishing Initial Balances

You picked your family very well. How smart of you to have had an uncle like your late, great uncle Harry—a thrifty bachelor of abundant means and no other living heirs.

Thanks to Uncle Harry's generous will, you were able to purchase a beach-front lot. It's not the world's greatest property; the view of the ocean is terrific, but the decrepit cottage is just too storm-battered for occupancy. "Might as well just tear down the existing cottage," you reason, "and build a new, modern one on the old foundation." That is what you decide to do, and your architect gets busy designing the new cottage to your specifications.

That weekend you just happen to tune in to a new episode of "This Old Money Pit," a home improvement program in which the host, Phil, and his carpenter, Sven, are dealing with the very same kind of rebuilding situation.

"Well, Sven," says Phil, "the new plans are here today, and the new cottage will be terrific. The owners will really love what the architects have come up with, even though the cost of renovation will surely put them into deep financial distress for the rest of their lives. But, hey, it's only money. Right, Sven?"

"Right, Phil," drones Sven. "And when you throw in the cost of fixing the foundation, they'll truly be ready for the poorhouse."

"What's with the foundation, Sven?"

"It's out of plumb on two sides, Phil. And those two sides will have to be rebuilt if we want the new building to be plumb and stable. There's no way you can square a superstructure if the foundation is out of alignment."

"I can't argue with that logic, Sven. The owners will just have to ante up another $40,000. But, hey, how do you like what the architects have done with the deck?"

As we complete the design and preparation phase, we find ourselves in a position analogous to the property owner in the story. The blueprints for the new inventory system are in hand; the right personnel have been trained to build and run it; but what kind of foundation will we build it on?

CALIBRATING INITIAL ON-HAND BALANCES

Once the inventorying process has been properly designed and put into place, a company has a mechanism capable of achieving its goal of at least a 95 percent inventory record accuracy. At this point it is necessary to establish initial on-hand and on-order balances. The reason is obvious: Prior to designing the inventory process, both of these records were inaccurate. This was determined when the starting point was measured (see Chapter 5). Nothing in the design process improved the accuracy of these existing balances. To implement the new inventorying process without first creating accurate starting balances would simply add and subtract accurate numbers to and from inaccurate balances. The results would be, of course, inaccurate records.

Establishing accurate initial balances is the second of our three-phase approach and is sometimes referred to as "calibrating the quantities." From an engineering point of view, this is an exact analogy. There are three approaches to calibrating initial record balances:

1. Taking physical inventories

2. Cycle counting

3. Systematic physical counting

All three approaches work with varying success depending on the environment. Each involves a lot of hard work, but each is basically straightforward. Before these approaches are described and critiqued, however, it is important to recognize that a calibration process must meet two critical criteria:

1. *Accuracy.* It is vital that the process of calibrating initial record balances be, in fact, accurate. Since its purpose is to create reliable initial balances that the inventory process can build on, the foundation provided in this activity must be solid.

2. *Quick.* Psychologically, it is important that the calibration process be performed on all records very quickly. Four weeks is the maximum amount of time that should be allowed for this process. One to three weeks is ideal, but absolutely *never* more than four weeks. The calibration process is a signal to everyone that a new way of doing business is being introduced with respect to inventory—one with particular attention to accuracy. If the calibration drags on for three to six months, the impact on the behavior of the personnel involved is diluted to the point of nullifying the effort.

THE PHYSICAL INVENTORY

The most common and traditional approach to establishing initial on-hand balances is to take a physical inventory of all the parts in stock and in the work-in-process. This means mobilizing a large group of people to physically comb through every aisle of every stockroom and WIP area—like so many census takers—counting every inventory item. The records representing these quantities are then set equal to this physical count.

This approach definitely meets the "quick" criterion but almost without exception falls short of the "accuracy" criterion. Contrary to the prevailing belief of most manufacturing and distribution managers, a physical inventory is seldom accurate in practice. It is far from being a "cure-all" for errant inventory records. To understand why, let us consider the typical company's attempt to conduct a physical inventory.

*   *   *

Hot Wheels Bicycle Manufacturing Company decided to conduct a physical inventory. Its records were so unreliable that management felt it necessary to order a complete count of every sprocket, wheel, shifter, spoke, length of steel tubing, and ball bearing in the place.

To minimize disruption of normal manufacturing activities, Hot Wheels decided to recruit a crew large enough to blitz the place over a weekend. The stockroom manager was unable to schedule all the stockroom attendants because their union contract prohibited mandatory overtime, and so he asked other areas of the company for volunteers. Attracted by the prospect of overtime, four stock attendants, four assemblers, three janitors, a cook from the cafeteria, and one security guard volunteered to fill out the inventory crew. Some could work only one of the two days.

The stockroom manager planned to break his weekend crew into small teams, each being assigned a number of aisles. The stockroom manager and his assistant planned to supervise, assist, and deal with any problems that might arise. They were optimistic that the inventory would go smoothly and produce an accurate result. Counting parts is not, they reasoned, rocket science. Anyone who could count and write could do the job.

After fifteen minutes of instructions by the stockroom manager on Saturday morning, the teams began their tasks. By that afternoon, everything seemed to be going well. In fact, the stockroom manager was surprised that almost no one came to him with problems. By three o'clock, however, he discovered that two of his teams had not followed his instructions. Instead of counting all the chain derailliers in aisle 6, one of the teams was counting the boxes these derailliers came in—and some boxes contained two derailliers while others contained three. The other team had misidentified a number of expensive components; they had confused the special-alloy pedal cranks with the standard steel models, which looked practically identical. No one was sure how many of these parts had been misidentified during the inventory. Whether the other teams were doing a good job or not was anyone's guess.

The inventory manager knew that there would not be sufficient time for these teams to recount the problem parts. He would have to let it ride and hope to do a recount sometime the next week.

The experience of Hot Wheels Bicycle is not farfetched. Physical inventories have many problems. It is important to note that the process of physically counting parts does not produce inaccurate counts. On the contrary, the method and personnel involved are most often the culprits. Typically, a physical inventory is conducted against sharp time constraints, usually one or two days, and when trade-offs are required between accuracy and finishing the job on time, accuracy usually finishes second. For the manager in charge of conducting an inventory, inaccuracies will not be immediately obvious, but not finishing the job on time will be seen by all.

Main Problems with Physical Inventories

Although not the recommended approach, a physical inventory to recalibrate on-hand balances will work provided that the parts are properly identified and accurately counted. The biggest deterrents to success are the problems that personnel have in properly identifying parts, correctly recording the units of measure (dozen, gallons, pair, and so forth), and accurately counting the items themselves. These fundamental problems are only compounded by time constraints and lack of training.

Improving the Accuracy of Physical Inventories

To assure an accurate physical inventory, three principles must be adhered to:

1. *Only people knowledgeable about the parts being counted should be assigned the task.* This means a stockroom that contains only fabricated parts should be counted only by someone familiar with fabricated parts. Should the stockroom contain both fabricated and assembly-type parts, then personnel familiar with both types of parts needs to be part of that counting team. It cannot be overemphasized that the biggest problem with the physical inventory of parts is parts identification. The ideal

personnel to bring to this task is the stockroom staff itself. If others must be brought in, they need to be familiarized with the parts they will be counting, how the storage areas are organized, and what units of measure are assigned.

2. *Everything should be counted twice*—and the time to count twice should be built into the schedule. This rule embraces the reasonable assumption that the counters will make mistakes. To assure that the second counter does not simply make the same errors, the second count should be made by another team.

3. *Everyone involved with the physical inventory must receive instruction.* Counting parts might not be rocket science, but no good result will come of this laborious process if personnel are not (a) sensitized to the importance of absolute accuracy, (b) familiarized with the process of counting and recording, and (c) given access to authoritative help when they encounter problems or ambiguities.

Following these three principles will reduce the amount of error in the physical inventory.

Teams and Counting Cards

A second count can be done simultaneously by utilizing two separate counting teams, each starting at opposite ends of the stockroom. One team, Team A, should start in the first aisle, and the other team, Team B, should start in the last aisle. They should work toward each other and eventually pass each other. In this manner, when the process is completed, each part in each location will have been counted twice, once by Team A and once by Team B. Both teams should count "blind" with respect to each other; that is, neither team should know what the record balances are for each part, nor should either one know the counting results of the other team. In this case, blind means with respect to parts identification, location, and quantity.

To accomplish this task, two sets of count cards, labeled A and B, should be used. Each card needs two sections, separated by a perforation. A control number should be identically printed on both portions of the card. Figure 6-1 presents just such a card. Note that the left-hand portion has no space for any data to be entered; all data will be written on the right-hand portion. When a part is counted, the left-hand portion is separated from the count card and left with the parts. The right-hand portion is filled in with the following information and submitted to the physical inventory coordinator:

Part Number (P/N)

Part Description

Quantity (Qty)

Location

Unit of Measure (U/M)

Date

Counter's Name, Initials, or Employee/Clock Number (Emp)

Figure 6-1   Physical Count Charts for Teams A and B

843-A		843-A
		Description _____
		P/N _____ Qty _____
		Location _____ U/M _____
		Date _____ Emp _____

621-B		621-B
		Description _____
		P/N _____ Qty _____
		Location _____ U/M _____
		Date _____ Emp _____

Both teams perform the same function in the same way. Thus, when all the parts have been counted, there should be two audit stubs on each of the counted part numbers—one stub from Team A and one stub from

Team B. The physical inventory coordinator must then match up all the data portions of the tickets. The goal is to have no mismatches or single tickets. If a mismatch or single ticket exists, the parts in question must be immediately recounted by a third team—Team C—for the purpose of reconciling the discrepancy between Teams A and B. Only after each ticket has a matching count can the data be loaded into the records.

Users of this approach must recognize that it has one important drawback: The stockroom must be closed for normal receiving and issuing activity during the counting process.

The Central Audit Team

A central audit team must be available to all counting teams throughout this process. The major concern is not auditing the counting but auditing the data to ensure that it is legible and written in the correct format. Of particular concern are the locations and units of measure. A small amount of freelancing by those entering the data on the counting cards can make it virtually impossible to match the data portion of the cards. The audit team should also encourage the counting teams to stack or arrange parts as they count. This makes the second counts by the other team much easier.

Entering the Counting Data

Updating the on-hand balances with the new data should take place immediately after the counts are matched. Only then can the newly designed inventory process have a meaningful chance for success. In all situations, it is desirable to start picking and receiving parts as soon as the stockroom opens.

This same approach can be used to count work-in-process inventory. In these areas, however, the audit stubs are attached to the manufacturing order.

Despite the drawbacks, physical inventories continue to be used by companies when they establish initial balances. It should be clear from this discussion that these drawbacks can be minimized only by giving considerable attention to personnel, their training in the process, double counting, and allowing sufficient time to do the job right.

CYCLE COUNTING

Cycle counting is the process of selecting certain members of a population, called a sample, and measuring a feature of that sample. That measurement is then inferred to be a parameter of the population. The "cycle" in cycle counting refers to the methodology of systematically moving through the entire population over time. Thus, all the members of a population will eventually be part of a sample.

When cycle counting is used to establish initial on-hand record balances, it usually is viewed as a physical inventory spread over an extended period of time. Normally, this process is accomplished by the computer's selecting which parts are to be counted and when. The computer cycle counting program is written to select each part once through the calibrating period. Some randomness is included in this logic to provide some sense of overall inventory record accuracy on an ongoing basis.

Speeding the Cycle Counting Process

The difficulties with calibrating initial record balances through cycle counting are the time required to count all the parts and the fact that it does not provide a clean starting point. Calibrating the records using cycle counting can take six to eight weeks, depending on the size of the stockroom and the number of people doing the counting. This violates one of the two requirements for establishing initial balances: quickness. Another significant drawback is that normal stockroom activities are happening concurrently with the calibration process. Psychologically, this method provides the personnel in the stockrooms with a sluggish, indeterminate starting point—not a desired effect or an effective springboard for launching a newly designed inventory process.

To partially overcome this time problem, cycle counting activity should be focused on one stockroom at a time. In this way, each individual stockroom can be done more quickly, and the personnel operating those stockrooms know when their parts have been completely calibrated. Increasing the cycle counting work force until all the balances have been calibrated will also move the process along more quickly. The quantity of parts counted per day per cycle counter should be very high.

Updating Record Balances

When a part is identified and counted by the cycle counter, this informa-tion and the date should be entered into the inventory record-keeping system. Once each balance has its date equal to or later than the cycle counting start date, the calibration process has been completed. It must be recognized that if software logic is selecting the parts to count, it will miss any part that has been erroneously left unrecorded; that is, any part physically on hand but not on the record. It cannot be selected for cycle counting since it does not exist as far as the computer is concerned. A cumbersome but workable method to locate these parts is to have the cycle counters attach a colored marker or label to each part number and location as it is counted. When the records indicate all parts have been counted, the stockroom is then physically checked for any parts not bearing a count marker or label. This method of calibration assumes that all parts are being accurately received. It eliminates the need to cycle count them for calibration purposes if, and only if, there is no previous on-hand balance in the record file. In practice, this means that when a quantity of parts is received, the on-hand balance must be checked. If that part shows a cycle count date within the calibration period, a marker or label should be attached to the material when it is stored. This also holds true if parts are being stored with piece count by multiple locations and are not being consolidated with previous uncounted bal-ances. It is suggested that a cycle count date be entered for these parts when they are put on location. In all other situations, the parts are to be stored and fall subject to the cycle counting calibration process.

In the hands of highly skilled practitioners, cycle counting can be successfully used to calibrate on-hand balances. For most, however, it tends to be not only a drawn-out process but messy and confusing. It is not the recommended approach. Cycle counting is an important and powerful tool, but its highest use, as we will see in the following chapter, is in maintaining accurate records once they are established. What is needed is a calibrating method that more fully meets the requirement of both accuracy and quickness. In developing that superior method, we draw on the better of the two approaches we have already reviewed.

SYSTEMATIC PHYSICAL COUNTING

The recommended approach to establishing initial record balances is to use what we call "systematic physical counting" methodology. This combines the best features of the physical inventory and cycle counting, incorporating the quickness of the physical inventory and the accuracy of cycle counting. It can be correctly argued that this approach is really a type of physical inventory—but a very special hybrid. It takes full advantage of the software feature called "piece counts by multiple locations." Briefly, this is the ability, recordwise, to capture both the location and quantity of parts, as shown in Figure 6-2. This is particularly important here because systematic physical counting takes us from one location to the next in a logical sequence, with a rebalancing of the record quantities as we go.

Figure 6-2

Part Number	On-hand Quantity	Location
1234	90	YA06B1
	25	YG01D4
	35	YH04A2
TOTAL	150	

Inventory record software either has the multiple location feature or it does not. Since it is very difficult, if not impossible, to maintain inventory record accuracy ≥ 95 percent when storing inventory in multiple locations without this feature, any firm that does not have it must use single locations. Regardless of the record-keeping capabilities, systematic physical counting is always done the same way. The steps to systematic physical counting are as follows:

1. Specifically identify a *geographical segment* to be counted. Segments in this context can be aisles, bins, racks, or areas that can be completely counted in one day. Never start a segment that cannot be

finished in one time period. For illustration purposes, let us designate the geographical segment to be counted today as aisle "A" in stockroom "Y."

2. Using the multiple location capabilities, electronically change the location of all parts located in aisle "A" of stockroom "Y" (YA___) to location "START." The parts are not physically moved. However, a stock status report would show them all in location START. The START location indicates that the parts have not yet been calibrated. Part number 1234 with 90 pieces on hand in aisle "A" would now appear as in Figure 6-3.

Figure 6-3

Part Number	On-hand Quantity	Location
1234	90	START
	25	YG01D4
	35	YH04A2
TOTAL	150	

3. The counters then count every part in every location in aisle "A." When a part is counted in a specific location, a *stock-to-stock* transfer transaction is entered, moving the number actually counted from location START to the specific location in which the parts were found. Thus, if 88 pieces of part number 1234 were counted in location YA06B1, the stock-to-stock transfer would be made to move 88 pieces from START to YA06B1 on the records. The results would appear as in Figure 6-4.

A review of the records indicates that 88 pieces of 1234 have been calibrated because they have a detailed location in the geographical segment that has been counted. The 2 pieces in START are, of course, dubious and reflect the accuracy of the population prior to calibration.

After aisle A is counted, all parts in the first geographical segment would have detailed locations. Obviously, as aisles are calibrated, they would have to be designated as such with some type of marker to indicate that the records have been calibrated. Ribbons or small floor

Figure 6-4

Part Number	On-hand Quantity	Location
1234	2	START
	88	YA06B1
	25	YG01D4
	35	YH04A2
TOTAL	150	

stanchions can serve this purpose. Once an area is calibrated, receipt and issue transactions must have their detailed locations included on the transactions. The calibrated areas should remain accurate because ongoing cycle counting is now applicable.

When comparing Figures 6-3 and 6-4, note that the total on-hand quantity for part 1234 remains unchanged through the entire counting process. No adjustments are made until all locations are counted. This relieves the pressure to finish the counts very quickly and adjust the balances, which often accompanies a physical inventory. Should part 1234 be expensive or critical, the cycle counters have the option of recounting locations YA06B1, YG01D4, and YH04A2 before zeroing out location START. A recount could also take place immediately should a large or costly discrepancy from the record balance be discovered.

At some point, all quantities in location START for all parts must be zeroed. One source of comfort to the finance department often comes when calculating the dollar value of all these final START quantities, which are items that cannot be accounted for. It is quite common to have the sum of these be very small because the pluses cancel out the minuses.[1] The net of these pluses and minuses is the start-up cost and should be charged to an inventory adjustment account. Figure 6-5 reflects positive and negative balances on hand in START.

---

[1] Although it is not recommended to allow the inventory system to carry negative balances on an on-going basis (see Chapter 4, software considerations), this feature is very helpful when establishing initial balances. We recommend allowing the software to accommodate this situation initially, but not on an ongoing basis.

Figure 6-5

Part Number	On-hand Quantity	Location
1234	2	START
	88	YA06B1
	25	YG01D4
	35	YH04A2
TOTAL	150	
1255	−4	START
	26	YA01C4
	12	YB01A3
TOTAL	34	

Part number 1255 in Figure 6-5 reflects a total of 34 pieces on hand. On the surface, one might argue that this is an obvious error. One must recognize, however, that before the calibration process began, the total record on hand was 34. The adjustment will not be seen until the START quantities are zeroed.

Through this systematic process, segment by segment, the on-hand balances are calibrated. As we will detail in Chapter 7, ongoing cycle counting, supplemented with problem-solving sleuthing, can then be used on the entire population of part numbers to keep their records accurate. Naturally, the systematic physical inventory method works best when it is implemented by people who really know what they are doing. Only well-trained, knowledgeable personnel should be used. The best candidates are cycle counters; next best, stock attendants. Both sets of individuals are knowledgeable about the parts being counted and the parts location and labeling system.

Systematic physical counting is a superior—and thus, recommended—approach to establishing initial balances for a number of important reasons:

- It is more accurate.

- It is quicker.

- It can be employed and confined to just one section while the rest of the stockroom and other locations operate as usual.

- It requires fewer people.

CALIBRATING ON-ORDER BALANCES

Thus far, we have considered only calibration of on-hand inventories, but the same techniques can be applied to on-order inventories. On-order balances must be loaded into the material management software (MRP II), and if inaccurate, they will be responsible for creating invalid material plans.

The on-order records that concern us most are purchase orders and manufacturing (or work) orders. These orders normally carry three balances: original order quantity, quantity received, and balance due quantity. The balance due quantity is the number on which we should focus. With manufacturing orders, the component allocation balances must be checked and calibrated as well.

In general, the balances due for on-order quantities are more forgiving than the on-hand balances because all will eventually be closed when their parts are received. Therefore, they tend to purge themselves over a period of time. Very few companies have purchase orders or manufacturing orders that stay open for more than a year, and these few orders are easily checked.

Purchase Orders

Purchase orders are normally the easiest on-order balances to review and calibrate. Review consists of comparing the balance due on the purchase order file to the balance due communicated to the supplier. In other words, does the purchase order quantity in our file agree with the quantity requested from the supplier? When the purchasing system can properly translate the balance due on file to a printed purchase order, it is not necessary to review those orders unless the order has been filled, in which case the order quantity and the balance due quantity should be the same. It gets complicated only when a portion of an open purchase order is filled. For example, your company may have an open purchase order with XYZ Company for 100 sprockets. If all 100 are received at once, the problem of review and recalibration of the records is straightforward; if XYZ Company sends only 40, then the job is more complicated. In these cases, overdue or partially filled purchase orders should be separated from the entire open purchase order population, and the suppliers contacted for confirmation of the balances due. This is the job of the buyers (purchasing agents, planner/schedulers, or vendor/scheduler) who initiated the orders; it is not a job for temporary inventory employees.

Additionally, the review process should be sized and monitored. That is, the number of orders requiring review should first be determined and then reduced as the orders are checked. Initially, each buyer will have a number of orders to review. These should be divided by supplier and a single contact made to verify all balance due quantities. Separating the orders in this manner organizes the work and makes it measurable. Again, this process needs to be both quick and accurate. All open purchase orders should be reviewed and calibrated within one month.

Manufacturing Orders

Reviewing and calibrating open manufacturing orders is slightly more difficult than doing the same for purchase orders. As with purchase orders, the balance due quantities are the focus of attention. Additionally, with manufacturing orders, their allocations, quantities, and the part numbers of items (components) issued to the order must be checked.

Manufacturing orders with no activity need not be checked (assuming, of course, that the manufacturing order system correctly establishes allocations). These include manufacturing orders queued for release to the stockroom or to the factory, and those in the stockroom queued for picking but not yet picked. Orders on the factory floor do need to be reviewed; and those that have been partially filled require the greatest scrutiny.

Like the purchase order file, the task of reviewing manufacturing orders must be sized, monitored, and assigned to the material planners, schedulers, and/or production supervisors in the factory who "own" these orders. They need to physically check their own orders. Their first concern should be with manufacturing orders in the primary, or initial, work centers. These have priority because they are just starting their manufacturing processes. Manufacturing orders in the finishing work centers should have lower priority because they will be completed soon and tend to purge themselves upon receipt into stock.

Physical checking of manufacturing orders should include the number of pieces being made on the order as well as the component pieces issued to it. In cases of a single piece part, this is very simple and straightforward. An example would be an order for a machined casting. The manufacturing order may call for 100 finished pieces, starting with 100 raw castings. The review process should locate the order in the factory and check that 100 castings were issued to the order and that all 100 are physically in process. Should there be only 90 castings reported issued to the order and 90 pieces in process, no calibration is required. (Note: In this case, there should be allocations open for 10 castings for this order.) If the quantity of castings reported issued and the quantity physically located in process differ, and if the discrepancy is not accounted for with a scrap, return-to-stock, receipt, or other transaction, an adjustment must be made to correct and properly reflect the situation. Obviously, this review process becomes much more difficult when the manufacturing order calls for the manufacture of a complex assembly with many components and stages of manufacture. Nonetheless, the review process is the same.

A major effort may be required in calibrating manufacturing orders when a company has operated for several years with informal systems. The biggest challenge is to identify and locate open manufacturing orders. In this environment, it is common to find orders that are on file, several months or years past due, and physically nonexistent. These must be purged from the open manufacturing order file. It is absolutely imperative that each and every manufacturing order on file be physically located and identified. Any manufacturing order that cannot be physically located must be deleted from the open order file. Likewise, those manufacturing orders located but not on file must be added to the file or physically destroyed. Should a manufacturing order physically exist with components but not be on file, a decision has to be made whether to load it on file or destroy it. If the decision is not to load the order on the open order file, the order must be destroyed and the components returned to stock or scrapped. If the decision is to load the order on the file, it must be loaded in such a way as to avoid the creation of new allocations. Most manufacturing control software packages accommodate this with a "rework type" order. Rework type orders do not generate allocations because they are expected to be added manually.

ON TO THE NEXT PHASE

Once the calibration process has been successfully completed, inventory record accuracy should rise above the 95 percent level. The first two phases of the inventory record accuracy program—design and preparation, and establishing initial balances—are thus complete. Those individuals who participated in these two phases should be made aware of the progress made. What follows is the process by which that high level of accuracy can be maintained. We have already been briefly introduced to that process: cycle counting.

Chapter 7

Phase III: Cycle Counting

Gizmo, Inc., the manufacturing company introduced in Chapter 2, had its fill of production problems stemming from parts stock-outs and other inventory-related problems. The final blow came when 1,200 units of a $120 part were discovered in a secondary storeroom. The firm's inventory records did not even recognize the existence of these parts. Since the parts were old and obsolete, they could not be returned or used, and had to be written off as a total loss. With the full backing of top management, the firm decided to adopt an accuracy improvement program and at the same time set a goal of 95 percent or better for its inventory record accuracy.

Personnel assigned to the inventory record problem did everything recommended thus far in this book, and they did everything very well. In March 1992, they began to measure the accuracy of their current records and found—with tolerances set arbitrarily at ±5 percent on all parts—that the firm's accuracy was an abysmal 52 percent. Almost as many "misses" as "hits."

No wonder they were showing hundreds of some parts on hand when, in fact, the cupboard was bare. The stockroom manager had the art department make up a large poster, which he hung on his office door. In bold letters it proclaimed:

INVENTORY RECORD ACCURACY, MARCH 1992: 52%
INVENTORY RECORD ACCURACY GOAL: *95% OR BETTER* BY AUGUST 1992

111

Over a period of five months, Gizmo personnel in finance, purchasing, manufacturing, and inventory management designed a new system for inventory records, complemented by reorganized stockroom facilities, staff training, and inventory records software capable of tracking parts in multiple locations.

Once the fine-tuning of the new system was finished, stockroom personnel conducted a complete inventory of the plant using the "systematic physical inventory" methodology described in Chapter 6.

It was now July 1, 1992, and the inventory manager could look at the poster on his door and say with certainty that his recalibrated inventory records were now well above 95 percent accurate. Gizmo had met its goal. Or had it? August 1992 was still a month away. With the thousands of transactions bound to take place in July, and many of his stockroom personnel heading off on vacation, how accurate would those records be in August? Would record accuracy slip over time?

Bringing inventory record accuracy up to a high level requires tremendous effort. This chapter provides the tools needed to maintain that level of accuracy.

SAMPLING AND INVENTORY RECORDS

Cycle counting is sampling—that is half of its definition. Sampling has a definite mathematical meaning. It is a technique in which certain members of a population (the sample) are selected, and a feature of those members is measured. It is then inferred that this measurement is a characteristic of the population. Political pollsters, market researchers, quality specialists, and scientists all use sampling techniques to infer from a small, representative sample some characteristic of a much larger population. Sometimes this is done because it is the *only* practical way. Imagine a military ordnance manufacturer which needs to assure itself that its hand grenades will explode 99 percent of the time. A sure method of determining reliability would be to try each grenade; but the company's entire production would either go up in smoke or be scrapped as duds if this method were used. A more practical solution would be to test a sample of its production, and to infer from that sample the reliability of the remaining production.

In other cases, sampling has been shown to yield more accurate results than a survey of the entire population—and at much less cost. To understand how, consider a pollster hired to assess the political preferences of the citizens of California. The candidate paying for the poll wants to know what Californians are thinking *right now;* he wants a snapshot of voter opinion. A poll that questioned every registered voter in that state would require months and would cost the candidate a fortune. Even worse, it would not be accurate because over the course of the months required to conduct the survey, voter sentiment would be changing.

Figure 7-1 shows a population of 100 members (m). Let us suppose that each of these members is an inventory record of the Gizmo company and that the entire population of 100 represents all the company's inventory records. If we wanted to know the accuracy of the firm's inventory records, we could do it in one of two ways.

Figure 7-1   Population of 100 Members (m)

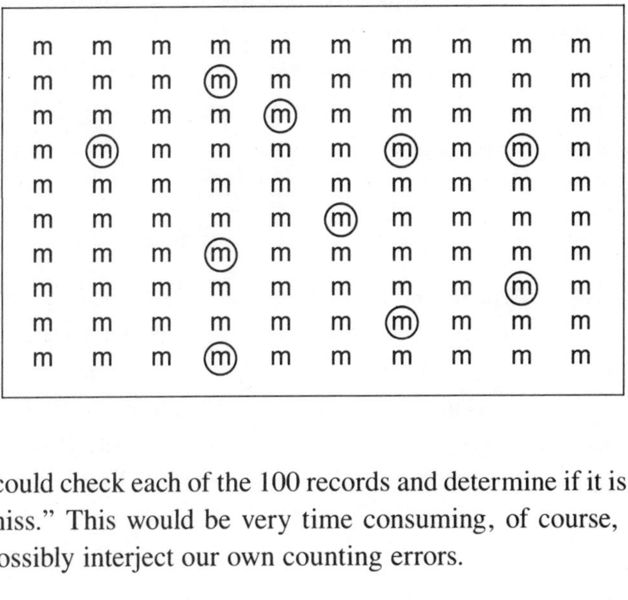

1. We could check each of the 100 records and determine if it is a "hit" or a "miss." This would be very time consuming, of course, and we could possibly interject our own counting errors.

2. We could select a sample of 10 members. We might do this by throwing 10 darts at Figure 7-1; the ones we hit—the circled m's— would then be in our sample. We could check each of these carefully and infer from this sample the accuracy of the total population of records. If we were to find that 60 percent of the sample records were accurate, we could infer that 60 percent of all of Gizmo's records were accurate. This would save us a great deal of time. But would a sample of 10 records give us a true picture of all 100 inventory records?

Two characteristics of a sample determine how well that sample represents the entire population. The first is the size of the sample relative to the population. If the sample size is extremely large, say 90 of the 100 in Figure 7-1, it would likely be an excellent reflection of the population. Conversely, a tiny sample, let's say just 1 of our 100 Gizmo records, might not be as representative and thus would not allow us to make inferences about the population with any sense of confidence.

The second and equally important characteristic of the sample is its *stability*. That is, if a sample produces a particular result, and when the sample size is increased it continues to produce the same result, the sample has stability and can be assumed to be a reliable representation of the population. This is an important characteristic when the population size is unknown or extremely large. This characteristic allows political pollsters to confidently predict election outcomes with only a small percentage of the ballots reported.

INFERENCES

Two important inferences can be made when sampling, or cycle counting, inventory. The first and most obvious is that the accuracy of the sampled records approximates the accuracy of the population of records. This inference is usually made when the records are being used to place a financial value on assets held in inventory, or to determine the ability of the inventory records to support a material planning system. The size of the sample relative to the population and the stability of that sample can be used to determine just how closely the sample approximates the population.

The second and more important inference concerns types of errors found in the inventory records of the sample and their causes. If we find certain errors and, with a little sleuthing, uncover their causes, we might reasonably expect to find the same errors in other records. Learning the causes allows us to take corrective measures, both in the sample and in the population. For example, we open three boxes—each marked that it contains one gross (144 pieces)—from a specific supplier. We find that one box contains 128 parts and the other two each contain 130. We can infer the probability that other boxes from this supplier are likewise short-packed. It can be further inferred that if we found the cause of the short-packing and had the supplier correct it, subsequent shipments from the supplier would not be short-packed.

These two inferences make cycle counting the most effective tool in maintaining record accuracy.

Cycle counting is very useful in measuring inventory accuracy, but its highest value may be in finding errors, and from those errors their causes. It is unacceptable to simply use cycle counting to find and correct errors. This would treat the symptoms but not the disease. In the long run, the discovery and treatment of the *cause* of errors are much more important. [1]

Correcting errors discovered through sampling also destroys important clues to the causes of those errors; this is no different from the novice detective "tidying up" a crime scene before the lab experts arrive to scour the area for clues and evidence. Both eliminate useful information. For example, if a shelf quantity for a part is found to exceed the record quantity and the cycle counter simply adjusts the record to reflect the actual amount, the counter has eliminated clues to the source of the error. Finding more of a part on the shelf than the record states

---

[1] This method of finding variances between a "standard" and actual performance or output and seeking their causes is the very basis of the philosophy of Continual Improvement. Variances are not just annoyances that require correction, they are indicators that something in the process is out of whack. And what is out of whack will usually stay that way until the cause is found and corrected.

may be an indication that a stock attendant is mistakenly pulling stock from an adjacent bin while reducing the records for the part in question; thus, there are plenty on the shelf and few in the inventory record. A little detective work might find the reverse record problem with respect to an adjacent part—too many in the record, too few on the shelf. This would confirm that the stock attendant is the probable cause of the error.

In the example just discussed, the initial impulse to correct the record and move on would merely have corrected the current error; changing the behavior of the stock attendant would correct future errors. This is one of the ways in which cycle counting maintains the accuracy of the entire inventory record system.

All cycle counting techniques are the same with one exception: the method used to select a sample from its population.[2] The four types of cycle counting discussed here are *control group cycle counting, random sample cycle counting, ABC cycle counting,* and *process control cycle counting.*

CONTROL GROUP CYCLE COUNTING

In the scientific community, control groups are used to detect changes or side effects caused by some activity under testing. For example, if a drug company receives the go-ahead to use a new formulation on humans, it will first give the drug to a small control group of patients and then closely monitor that group for reactions to the drug. The term "control" implies that factors other than the drug are controlled, or kept the same, so that the observed changes in the patients can be ascribed directly to the new drug and to no other influence.

Control group cycle counting is used for a similar purpose—for proving out the new design of the inventory process. It is the only form of cycle counting not truly used to measure inventory record accuracy. Control group cycle counting entails counting the same parts in the same locations repeatedly within a very short time frame. If the design of the inventory process has flaws, they should be observable in the

---

[2] Mathematicians stress this selection process. For our purposes, however, the selection process does not seem to make any significant difference in result, provided the selection method is not seriously biased toward any one small group or part.

control group of parts. The parts counted are the "control group." The purpose of this procedure is to verify a change in the process by reducing the time between cycle counts of a part, thereby facilitating the sleuthing or finding of errors and their causes. When an extended period of time elapses between counts for a part and then an error is found, there may be hundreds or thousands of candidates for the cause of the error. Reducing the time between counts also reduces the error exposure time, and the number of candidates can be more easily analyzed and corrected.

Control group cycle counting involves five steps:

1. Identify the control group.[3] A control group of 100 different part numbers in 100 different locations is recommended. These parts should represent a cross section of the inventory—that is, big and small parts, fast and slow movers, expensive and inexpensive, parts of different materials, and even bulk parts. A few of every category is best.

2. Count the control group. Do a careful count and ensure that all outstanding transactions on these parts are processed before moving to the next step.

3. Set the inventory records equal to the counts. Do not spend undue time or energy trying to reconcile or determine the causes of errors if count quantities and records are not the same. Simply set the two equal and proceed.[4] This done, the control group accuracy will be 100 percent.

4. After a three- to five-day interval (one week at the most), recount the control group in exactly the same locations.

5. Compare the recounts to the updated inventory records.

[3] Multiple stockroom/warehouses could result in multiple control groups.

[4] Should an error involving an expensive or critical part be found that requires determination of the cause, set it aside from the control group and select a replacement.

Outcomes and Remedies

In control group cycle counting, two knowns—the actual quantity and the record quantity—are set equal to each other the first time the group is counted (Steps 2 and 3). If the inventorying process is working correctly, they will remain equal in subsequent recounts (Steps 4 and 5). That would be the best of all possible outcomes. The next best outcome would be if the actual quantity and record quantity were unequal after only one transaction is made on the part number between counts. That one transaction would be the likely candidate for the error.[5]

The next best result would be to find a discrepancy between the record count and the physical count in the presence of two transactions on the part number. Both transactions are likely candidates as the cause of the error. As the number of transactions increases, the investigative work necessary to finding error causes becomes correspondingly more difficult. In fact, in some high-moving parts, so many transactions are reported against them in the course of a week that special steps must be taken to reduce them to a workable number; these include the requirement to count the control group on a daily or hourly basis.

The most troublesome situation occurs when the record quantity and the physical quantity are unequal *in the absence of any reported transactions*. Here the list of potential culprits is long, and tangible clues are virtually nonexistent. The error could be the fault of a careless stock picker, an error in the computer system, a failure to process a transaction, a transaction entered against the wrong part, and even theft. In these cases, the amount of investigative work necessarily increases.

Since control group cycle counting is performed to determine if the inventory process is well designed and working properly, a large number of the same type of error need not be collected before corrective action is taken. In fact, the cause of every error should be addressed very quickly.

Control group cycle counting is normally done prior to starting other

---

[5] It may not be the only candidate because the actual quantity could have been physically changed without a transaction being reported—as in the case of pilferage within the stockroom. This part could also have been physically increased or decreased and another part number inadvertently transacted.

types of cycle counting, and it is stopped once the process is proven. While some companies perform small control group cycle counting on a continuous basis, it is recommended that it be eliminated once other methods of cycle counting, more suited to measuring inventory accuracy, are introduced. The control group method should be kept in the "inventory record accuracy tool box" for use when the process is changed or when errors crop up that defy other means of detection.

RANDOM SAMPLE CYCLE COUNTING

This technique selects its sample from the population at random, thereby giving every member of the population an equal opportunity to be a member of the counting sample.

Visualize a population of 1,000 part numbers. If each number was written on a Ping-Pong ball and placed in a large bucket, the bucket thoroughly mixed, and 50 balls drawn by a blindfolded person, that sample would be considered random. This is the method used in most lottery drawings when chance determines the outcome. There is no inherent bias in the selection.

Random sample cycle counts are generally accepted as the best measure of inventory record accuracy if the sample has stability and if it is sufficiently large. Consider sampling 50 part numbers each working day (Monday through Friday) out of a population of 1,000 different part numbers, with the results arrayed in Figure 7-2:

Figure 7-2 Sampling 50 Part Numbers per Day for Accuracy

	Sampled	"Hits"	Accuracy (%)
Monday	50	50	100
Tuesday	50	49	98
Wednesday	50	48	96
Thursday	50	48	96
Friday	50	49	98
TOTAL	250	244	97.6

In this example, one-fourth of the total population (250 of 1,000) has been sampled during this short time, and the resulting 97.6 percent inventory accuracy can be confidently inferred to be representative of the total population because the sample size is large with respect to the total and because it has stability. Cycle counting each and every day ensures a large sample. If the sample does not have stability, the ability to infer its representation of the larger population is impaired.

There are two types of counting techniques using random samples of parts: the *constant population* technique and the *diminishing population* technique.

Constant Population Counting Technique

Recalling our large bucket of Ping-Pong balls—each labeled with a part number—imagine that we randomly pick 50 balls (our sample). We note the part numbers these balls represent and go into the stockroom to count them. With our counting and tabulating finished, the 50 balls are returned to the bucket where they are thoroughly mixed in with the other 950 balls. Figure 7-3a illustrates this procedure. When we go to pick another sample, each of the original 50 has an equal chance with the other 950 balls, of being picked. We are thus picking from a constant population every time we draw out a sample.

With our sample size of 50, we can cycl through the population every 20 days (1,000 part numbers ÷ 50 part numbers per day)—but only if we are not pulling out any of the balls previously sampled. With random sampling from a constant population, however, there is no assurance that all 1,000 parts would be sampled in this period—or any period! It is theoretically possible that some parts would never be sampled regardless

Figure 7-3a   Constant Population Counting

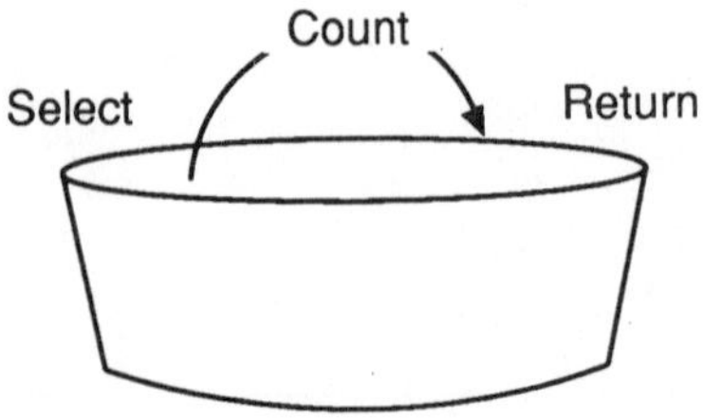

of how many samples were taken. Likewise, it is theoretically possible that one or more parts will become members of *every* sample.

The probability of either of these outcomes is extremely small, but it is sufficiently troublesome to induce many practitioners to move away from the constant population technique to an approach that draws its sample only from that portion of the population of part numbers that has not yet been picked—the diminishing population technique.

Diminishing Population Counting Technique

This method is similar to the first except that our Ping-Pong balls, once selected, are not returned to the bucket. Instead, they are held in another bucket until all the balls in the first bucket have been sampled. Figure 7-3b demonstrates this technique.

Using this technique, our second sample of 50 is drawn from the first bucket, which now contains a population of 950 balls. The third sample would be drawn from a population of 900. And so on.

This method guarantees that all members of the population will be sampled within 20 days. When the last sample of 50 balls is drawn from the first bucket, we will have zero balls in the first bucket and 1,000 in the second. After thoroughly mixing the contents of the second bucket, subsequent sampling will be made from it.

Diminishing Population Counting with Timing

While the diminishing population technique solves some of the problems inherent in the constant population method, it is not without its own problems. Only very long odds prevent the last ball picked from the first bucket from being the first ball picked from the second bucket. This

Figure 7-3b Diminishing Population Counting

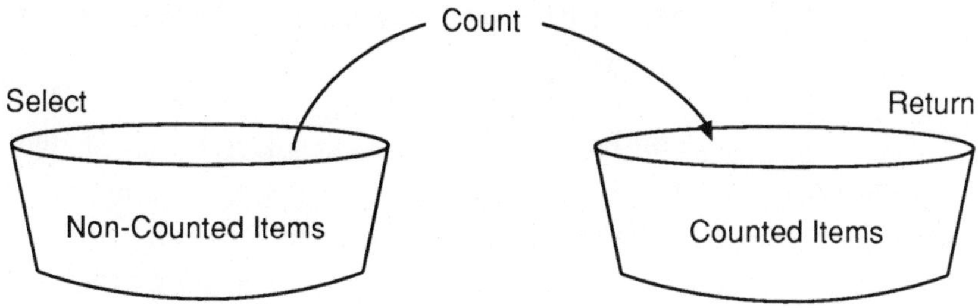

unlikely but possible occurrence would result in our counting the same part on two successive days. Even more disconcerting is the equal probability that the first ball picked from the first bucket will be the last ball picked from the second bucket. In this case, 39 days will have elapsed between counting of that part.

To avoid these undesirable possibilities, many practitioners employ a timing technique that dates the samples as they are withdrawn from the diminishing population bucket. If they want to cycle count the entire population every 20 days, as suggested earlier, the second round of sampling would follow the same order as that of the first; that is, all parts counted on day 1 would also be counted on days 21, 41, 61, and 81. Using this method, every specific part is counted at an elapsed time interval of exactly 20 days.

Which Method Is Best?

Provided that a reasonable number of samples is taken over a period of time, and provided that the sample results are stable, each of these methods of random sample cycle counting is highly effective in terms of measuring inventory record accuracy. Where they differ is in respect to the sleuthing aspects of cycle counting, such as:

- Constant population cycle counting contains the possibility that some parts may be repeatedly sampled while others may never be sampled.

- Diminishing population cycle counting assures that all parts are counted, but the regularity with which each part is counted is uneven as the counter cycles through the entire population of parts.

- The use of diminishing population cycle counting with timing assures that all parts will be counted and that they will be counted at equal and regular intervals.

None of the above effects are necessarily good or bad, but are simply offered as characteristics of each method. For instance, counting every single part is not required for accurate inventory records. In addition, counting parts at equal and regular intervals may or may not be helpful.

ABC CYCLE COUNTING

An alternative to random sample methods is ABC cycle counting. This method uses the Pareto Principle, which states that where there are many contributors to a result, a minority of the contributors account for a majority of the result. Salespeople have long held an understanding that they receive 80 percent of their revenues from 20 percent of their customers. This has been a popular rule of thumb across many industries even though few have tested the idea empirically.

The ABC cycle counting process puts an explicit bias on the samples to reflect the monies invested in inventory. Simply explained, the "A" class parts (the 20 percent of the parts that represents 80 percent of the total monies spent per year on inventory) are counted more frequently than the "B" and "C" class parts, which account for lesser expenditures. A typical distribution of inventory numbers is shown in Figure 7-4.

This method of cycle counting is designed to count the equivalent of 190 percent of the total stockroom parts each and every year, and the bias is toward those parts that generate the greatest annual expenditure.

Figure 7-4   Inventory Expenditures and Cycle Counting Frequency

Cost Class	Parts (% of total)	Dollars Spent (% of total)	Number of Parts	Times Counted	Total Counts/ Year	CC Effort[6] (% of total)
A	20	80	2,000	4	8,000	42
B	30	15	3,000	2	6,000	32
C	50	5	5,000	1	5,000	26
TOTAL	100	100	10,000		19,000	100

Implementing ABC Cycle Counting

The first task in performing ABC cycle counting is to develop the ABC cost classifications. The logic for this is straightforward, but it can be

[6] Eight thousand of 19,000 counts per year, or 42 percent of the total parts cycle counted per year, will be "A" cost classification parts; 6,000, or 32 percent, "B" parts; and 5,000, or 26 percent, "C" parts.

difficult if cost and usage data are not readily available. Computer-based planning systems have simplified this process by including these data and making them accessible for just such a task.

The data in the computer should be used to develop a report that lists the following information by part number:

- All part numbers
- Cost per part
- Estimated annual usage of each part
- Estimated annual dollar expense per part (part cost times estimated annual usage)

The parts are then listed in descending dollar amounts, that is, the part with the greatest annual expense at the top. A column next to each part's annual expenditure keeps a *cumulative* total, starting at the top (see Figure 7-5). The last line of this cumulative column represents the total annual inventory expense.

For the firm in Figure 7-5, then, an estimated $16 million will be spent on inventory. Part 6409 creates the greatest annual inventory expense, and part 5900 creates the least.

With a report of this kind, it is easy to identify the "A" parts by reviewing the cumulative dollar column and grouping those parts that account for 80 percent of $16 million ($12.8 million). A simple cross-check can be done by taking 20 percent of the total number of part

Figure 7-5   Annual Expenditure per Part (in Descending Order)

P/N	Cost per Unit ($)	Annual Usage (Estimated)	Annual Expense ($)	Cum. Total Annual Expense ($)
6409	185.00	10,500	1,942,500	1,942,500
1390	95.00	17,700	1,681,500	3,624,000
4317	105.00	15,714	1,649,970	5,273,970
.... other parts not shown				
5900	0.16	6,250	1,000	16,000,000

numbers and counting down the list by that number. These will seldom match exactly—that is, the top 20 percent of the parts will almost never account for precisely 80 percent of the total annual inventory cost—but they are often reasonably close. If this rule of thumb does not hold in a particular case, no major consequence will result. Companies often find that their cost/year part number distribution is 90 percent–10 percent or 80 percent–10 percent.[7] The Pareto Principle still holds: A few members of the population account for a major characteristic of the population. It is left to the practitioner to determine in these cases where the breaks between "A," "B," and "C" parts should be, and a great deal of time spent in determining these breaks is time wasted.

Selecting the Sample

With all parts classified by cost, the number of cycle counts per year needs to be determined; once that is determined, the number of people needed to do the counting can be established.

Gizmo, Inc. adopted the ABC method for its cycle counting, and the firm's parts distribution by class is presented in Figure 7-6. The inventory manager and his staff have set the frequency of counts for A, B, and C class parts, and from the information in the table, and the assumption of 250 working days/year, they can figure the number of part numbers that must be counted each day for each class.

Figure 7-6   Cycle Counting Requirements, Gizmo, Inc.

Cost Class	Part Numbers	Count Frequency	Counts per Year	Counts per Day*
A	2,000	4/Year	8,000	32
B	3,000	2/Year	6,000	24
C	5,000	1/Year	5,000	20
Total	10,000		19,000	76

* Assumes 250 working days/year.

[7] These two numbers need not add up to 100 percent. The second ratio merely states that 80 percent of the firm's annual inventory cost comes from 10 percent of the inventory parts.

The total of the ABC parts that require counting on each working day of the year is found here to be 76. Using his own experience with cycle counting, the Gizmo inventory manager figures that the average counter can handle 25 parts per day.[8] Thus, Gizmo needs three full-time cycle counters (76 counts/day ÷ 25 counts/day/counter = 3 counters), to count its 10,000 parts with the frequency determined by its management.

One of the flaws of this approach is that the more part numbers a firm has, the more cycle counters it requires. For example, suppose a firm has 30,000 or 50,000 part numbers. Stepping through the calculations to determine how many counters will be required produces some mind-boggling numbers; 30,000 part numbers translates into 228 counts per day, or 9 cycle counters (228 divided by 25 equals 9); 50,000 part numbers translates into 15 cycle counters.

Another flaw of ABC cycle counting is its bias toward counting those parts with the greatest annual expenditures. This may be logical from a strictly financial perspective. From a materials perspective, however, a "C" cost class part can just as easily prevent shipment of a product as can an "A" class part.

Process control cycle counting was developed, in part, to overcome both of these flaws.

PROCESS CONTROL CYCLE COUNTING

Many years ago the authors developed a method of sample selection and counting that addressed the inefficiencies of traditional forms of cycle counting. This method is called *process control cycle counting*. This method is controversial in theory but effective in practice. Before discussing this method, its prerequisites should be spelled out:

1. *Inventory records must have "piece count by multiple location" capability*, the characteristics of which were discussed in Chapter 5.

---

[8] Cycle counting 25 parts per day per cycle counter is, using random sample or ABC cycle counting, consistent with an informal survey of hundreds of attendees of Oliver Wight seminars on inventory record accuracy and MRP II over the decade of the 1980s.

Process control cycle counting is not feasible without this capability in the system. A records system that shows 100 pieces of a part and a list of possible locations is also inadequate. Nevertheless, this requirement can be met if the entire quantity of each part number is stored in only one location.

2. *An inventory record listing of all quantities in all locations for all parts is available to the cycle counter.* This is the stock status by location encountered in Chapter 5 (see Figure 5-12). The important point here is that the counter knows the quantity that *should be* in each location. Thus, we do not have a "blind count" situation.

With these two prerequisites met, cycle counting of samples then proceeds on the basis of three criteria: location, ease of counting, and obvious errors.

Location
The supervisor starts the process control cycle counting activity by assigning counters to specific areas. In a stockroom, these might be aisles, racks, or bins; in point-of-use storage, they might be specific work areas or cells.

Ease of Counting
As a counter counts a sample area, he or she verifies every part in every location. But when it comes to actual counting, only the easy parts are counted. Typically, these will be parts that are either low in quantity or packaged in ways that facilitate fast and easy counting.

When a large quantity of a particular part is found in a location—such as several thousand connectors—no physical count is made. Instead, the counter compares the large quantity to the inventory record to verify part identification, location, and order of magnitude. Thus, if a bin contains what appears to be a few thousand connectors and the record indicates a balance of 2,912, no physical count is made. This "eyeball assessment" is not considered a count; nor is the record considered accurate. It is simply considered a "skip."

Obvious Error

If a part is misidentified or mislocated, or if the order of magnitude of the quantities physically located and on the record are obviously mismatched, that part must be included in the sample and physically counted. For example, if a bin appears to have a few thousand connectors and the record shows a balance of 171, we would have an obvious order of magnitude error, and the connectors would have to be counted.

Using this method of cycle counting, we assess the overall inventory record accuracy using the formula discussed in Chapter 2. Here, however, we ignore all the "skips" and use only the part numbers and the number of accurate records in our calculation.

$$\text{Record Accuracy } (\%) = \frac{\text{Number of accurate records}}{\text{Number of part numbers counted}} \times 100\%$$

Concerns With the Process Control Cycle Counting Method

This method is not without its critics. Giving the individual cycle counter the freedom to select the sample parts—that is, giving the counter discretion to determine what is difficult to count—leads some to fear that the overall sample will be skewed in a way that misrepresents the overall population of parts. There is also the question of when the difficult-to-count parts get counted.

First, the issue of counting only the "easy-to-count" parts: Nothing in statistics differentiates the value of a specific sample by its quantity. A part whose quantity is 7,637 is no more or less statistically valuable than a part whose quantity is 1. The first is not 7,637 times more statistically significant. A sample member is a sample member and has equal weight with other sample members in representing the entire population, regardless of its respective quantity.

Second, a cycle counter's job is to count and reconcile records. The fact that a "blind count" is not made by one person and its reconciliation by another does not lessen the value of this method, unless one assumes that cycle counters will be rewarded for reporting accurate record percentages—even those fraudulently obtained. Parts and product inspectors are not required to conduct "blind" inspections. They approach their jobs, like the process control cycle counter, with the specifications in hand. We are not aware of a single company that asks its inspectors to examine a part without a specifications print in hand. No company expects its inspectors to measure the outside diameter of a part and then input that data into a computer for verification. On the contrary, the inspector is given the information ahead of time and is trusted to make the comparison of the designed part to the actual part. This practice should be just as valid when checking part number identification, location, and quantity on hand.

As for the argument that the counter will not count any parts, this can be easily monitored by recounting some of the part numbers reported by the cycle counter. Individual employees may be found who report erroneous count numbers, but this will surely be rare. Designing a cycle counting selection procedure around an implied distrust for the cycle counters will impose costly inefficiencies on the operation, and in the end, it is not the way to deal with untrustworthy employees. Those who are not satisfied with these responses to these arguments can still put process control cycle counting to good use. They can use it to find and fix the causes of errors and use random sample cycle counting or ABC cycle counting to measure inventory record accuracy.

Advantages of Process Control Cycle Counting

Statistical purists may find aspects of this method objectionable; however, these are overshadowed by a tremendous advantage: Process control cycle counting is *over 1,000 percent* more efficient than previously cited methods.[9] This fact has important ramifications for both costs and the number of parts that can be included in the sample size. The tremendous efficiency of the process control method means that we can—without greater cost—count and reconcile 10 to 20 times the part numbers in a given period of time than can random sample or ABC methods. This fact explains why the fear that hard-to-count parts will be

[9] Cycle counters at Hyster Company were able to count, on average, 320 part numbers per person per day using process control cycle counting. Using two individual counters, Hyster did 640 counts per day, 3,200 per week, and 12,800 per month. The result is that over one-third of the company's 30,000 part numbers were counted each month. Both counters could average only 26 counts per day when using random sample and ABC cycle counting.

bypassed is, for practical purposes, unfounded. So many part numbers are counted (the average is over 300 per cycle counter per day) that virtually all parts are counted in the course of a year—provided, of course, that a reasonable number of counters are used. Consider the part that never has an obvious error and is never easy to count. Theoretically, it may escape a physical count forever. Operationally, this outcome is highly unlikely. In one company that practiced process control cycle counting, a senior manager insisted that all parts be counted at least once every year. To honor that requirement, all parts that had not been counted within the previous twelve months were selected from the inventory records. Out of 30,000 total part numbers in the records, only 3 had not been counted at least once.

Since cycle counting serves the dual purpose of measuring inventory record accuracy and finding and fixing causes of errors, it is only logical to design the cycle counting methodology to excel at both. None of the methods discussed excels at both. Random sample cycle counting provides the best measure of inventory record accuracy; ABC is a close but biased second. Neither is as effective as process control cycle counting in detecting errors, enabling their causes to be corrected.

We inadvertently discovered this fact while simultaneously practicing both process control and random sample cycle counting on the same population for a period of two years. Process control cycle counting produced a continual stable inventory record accuracy of 97.2 percent ± 1/2 percent for that period. The parts population consisted of 30,000 part numbers. During the time of the observation, over 300,000 counts were made via process control cycle counting. To satisfy the company's general manager, the controller conducted a monthly random sample audit of 400 parts. Her sample measure of inventory record accuracy was 98.6 percent, again ± 1/2 percent. The results of both methods were consistent throughout the twenty-four-month period. Because both samples were extremely large with respect to the population and because they were both extremely stable, it was initially thought that two different characteristics of the population were being measured. This was not the case, however. It was eventually realized that both were a measure of inventory record accuracy. Random sample cycle counting was a pure measure of this. Process control cycle counting, on the other hand, was a biased measure, like ABC cycle counting. Where ABC has a bias toward those parts that have the greatest annual expenditure, process control cycle counting has a bias toward those parts with the greatest exposure to error.

The following situation illustrates this bias: 2,000 of part number 1764 are received and placed in location YB17A2. If no activity occurs in this location between the receipt of these parts and their cycle count, part number 1764 may or may not be counted depending on which method of cycle counting is used. Using the process control method, 1764 would assuredly be verified for parts identification and location, but most likely not actually counted. Thus, if the identification and location were correct and the record and actual quantities were reasonable, it would be skipped and not included in the sample.

Because the random sample method uses pure chance as its sample selection criteria, 1764 would be a *candidate* for the sample, but that would not assure its selection for counting. If it were selected, however, it would be counted. Process control would count this part only if it were obviously wrong, misidentified, or mislocated, or if it had an order of magnitude quantity mismatch. This puts a bias on process control's samples toward those parts with errors—which is, in fact, what we are most interested in. Additionally, if 1764 did not qualify to be sampled in this cycle of process control cycle counting because it did not have an obvious error, it would be counted at some future time when it became easy to count—that is, when its physical quantity was lowered through usage.

By the time that physical quantity has been reduced to the point where part 1764 is easy to count, it has been subject to at least two causes for error: its receipt into location YB17A2, and the one or many transactions that reduced its quantity to a lower level. Thus, the obvious error and ease of counting criteria of process control cycle counting force its sample to be biased toward those parts with the greatest probability of containing errors. This is a valuable attribute because it enhances one of the objectives of cycle counting: finding errors so that their causes can be determined and corrected.

The other objective of cycle counting is to measure record accuracy. Both the evidence produced earlier and the testimonials of many cycle counters attest to the outstanding ability of this method to measure accuracy.

WORK-IN-PROCESS CYCLE COUNTING

Up to this point we have concentrated on cycle counting on-hand balances in the stockroom. When it comes to work-in-process, the same concepts apply. Here, of course, we are addressing the open order file, not stock status. And instead of checking the storeroom, we are concerned with work-in-process areas. Selection of samples from these areas can be made by random sampling, ABC, process control, or via a control group.

In cycle counting work-in-process, we are attempting to verify that a manufacturing order exists and that all the components reported as issued to it are, in fact, with that order. There are two alternatives to accomplishing this:

1. Start with the open order listing and draw a sample. Then go onto the factory floor and compare the listing and the parts. Check for three things: (a) that the order is at the correct work center, (b) that the quantity due is correct, and (c) that the component(s) issued to it are correct.

2. Start in the work centers and select a work-in-process sample. Compare it to the records, exactly as in the first alternative.

The desire to cycle count work-in-process is symptomatic of a lack of good record-keeping in the stockroom. Running a tight ship in the stockroom will often alleviate the necessity of conducting cycle counting on the factory floor. This is particularly true when lead times are extremely short.

OTHER SAMPLING METHODS

In addition to the primary sampling techniques already mentioned, a number of others are being used by companies today:

High Frequency

This method is applied to parts used in great volume that are chronically out of balance with the records. The fast pace of transactions on these parts makes it difficult to determine the cause of error when many transactions occur between counts. For example, if 100 transactions occurred between our cycle counts, we would have 100 error candidates, thus making successful detective work difficult if not impossible. By counting more frequently—to the extreme of counting after every transaction—our sleuthing would likely find the source of error.

These are some times when counting is convenient or opportune:

Just Prior to Order Receipt or Issue

If an attendant sees that a part balance is low, a cycle count can be taken. To systematize this approach, one extra data field can be added to the picking documents signifying "remaining balance." These counts are called "opportunity counts" because stock attendants capture them during their normal receiving and issuing of inventory, essentially capturing a free cycle count.

Low Quantity

Yet another way to find easy counting is to target low-balance stock positions. This method is inherent in process control cycle counting. The computer can be used to identify and signal low quantities.

At Regular Intervals

Weekly, monthly, or annual counts can be mandated and triggered by the computer system.

Number of Transactions

As the number of transactions increases, so do the exposures to error. Some firms count parts at predetermined transaction numbers.

By Location

Cycle counting a specific rack, bin, or aisle.

Upon Request
Sometimes a scheduler or material planner will specifically request the count of a suspicious part number.

It is important to make a point here about computer-directed versus human-directed counting. Many available programs allow computers to tell people what to count and when—for instance, at time intervals, at receipt, or at order release times. But a computer is not a necessity; the many cycle counting techniques mentioned above make this clear. If a company has its on-hand balances in order and keeps them current, computer-directed counting is not necessary.

FINDING AND CORRECTING THE CAUSES OF ERRORS

After years of living with the problems associated with inaccurate inventory records, Gizmo, Inc. finally went through a long and thoughtful process of designing a new inventory system. It then recalibrated its initial balances to be sure that the new system was starting with accurate records. It also took the third step: It initiated a well-orchestrated plan for cycle counting.

A process control counting method was initiated. And it worked! Counters were discovering many errors, and they very efficiently corrected the records for those parts. Before long, the same part numbers would be found to be inaccurate again. To rectify this situation, the inventory manager ordered more frequent counting and even assigned several more personnel to cycle counting. With more frequent counts the errors were found to be smaller on each cycle—but the errors persisted nevertheless.

Gizmo was doing everything right—well, just about everything. In its cycle counting, the company was finding errors and recalibrating the records. This process kept the records aligned with the physical count for a while, but eventually they would become inaccurate. The company was also spending an inordinate sum on cycle counting.

Not surprisingly, the person in the firm who proposed a solution was the firm's quality specialist. Gizmo, as a manufacturer, had plenty of machine tools and milling devices in operation. In the past, these machines started out operating close to tolerances, but like all machines, they eventually began to lose their "true" as cutting tools, and other parts eventually wore out as workers on different shifts operated them. Errors would be detected, and as part of the quality program, their causes were tracked down by operators and engineers acting as detectives. Often the problem had nothing to do with the machines and everything to do with how they were being operated.

The quality specialist discovered that finding the cause of errors was his most important job. It was the only way to keep the machining and milling equipment operating within designated tolerances over any length of time. Errors would creep in but at a much slower pace than before.

The quality specialist helped the inventory manager recognize that he had the same problem. Finding and recalibrating the records was a short-term solution that did nothing to prevent errors from creeping back in. It also required the firm to do more counting to assure a reasonable level of accuracy at any given time.

Like quality management programs, the cycle counting system's greatest value is its ability to find errors so that their causes can be revealed and remedied. This is the most effective way to maintain record accuracy once it has been established.

The Fishbone Diagram

Not surprisingly, the field of quality offers a number of excellent techniques for exposing the root causes of problems. One of these is the cause-and-effect diagram, also known as an *Ishikawa* or *fishbone diagram* (Figure 7-7). This diagram gives everyone the opportunity to write down what they either suspect or know to be the source of a given problem.

To use the cause-and-effect diagram, the observed problem is described in the box at the "head" of the diagram: In Figure 7-7, the problem is a declining level of inventory record accuracy over time. The main branches of the diagram represent the possible causes. As a

Figure 7-7   Fishbone Diagram

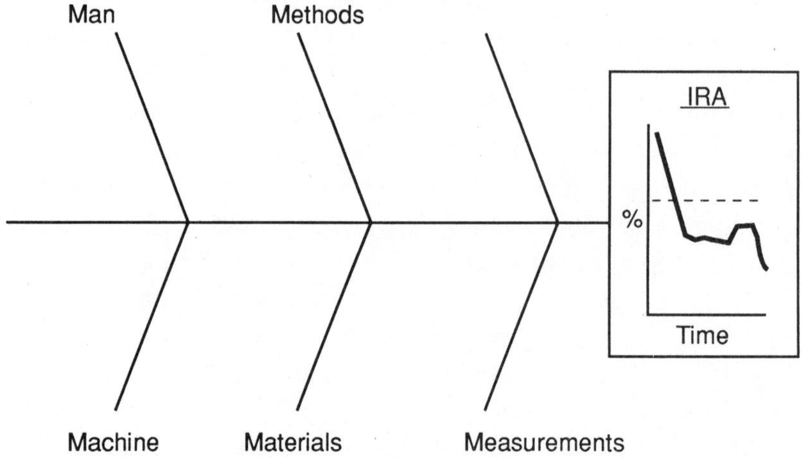

Man   Methods

Machine   Materials   Measurements

IRA

%

Time

starting point, these might be labeled with the five "m's": measurement, materials, method, machine, and man. Everyone involved with the problem is invited to attach his specific suspects to the appropriate branches. More than anything else, this technique encourages the kind of brainstorming that leads to the sources of error.

Pareto Analysis

Another excellent technique for ferreting out the causes of errors is *Pareto analysis.* We have already seen how the Pareto Principle can be used to segment part numbers by magnitude of annual expense. The same methodology can be used to segment errors by type and frequency. Figure 7-8 presents a Pareto chart that does this. Here, data about inventory inaccuracies by type and frequency are presented in a bar chart. We see at the top of the chart that the particular type of error most frequently occurs in the receiving of inventory. Other types of errors are arrayed in order of diminishing frequency. Each type of error can be further "decomposed" for examination. For instance, receiving of inventory is broken down here into four more specific sources of error. As the figure shows, each of these can in turn be decomposed. This process of analysis takes us progressively closer to the cause of the error. Experience indicates that the root cause of error is often four levels deep.

Figure 7-8   Pareto Analysis

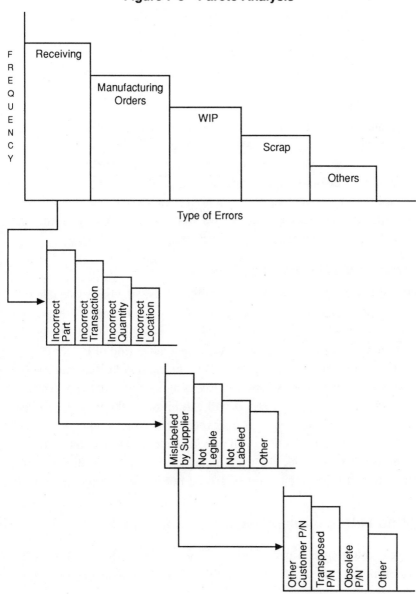

Pareto analysis is valuable in that it clearly indicates the greatest and lesser types of errors in our system, and from this it becomes clear where sleuthing attention should be focused: at the type of error that causes the most frequent problems. [10] Once the cause of that type of error is discovered and eliminated, the next most fruitful area is investigated.

Flip Charts

Still another effective and very simple approach to resolving errors is to gather data by means of a flip chart. Set up the chart in the stockroom with a pen attached and encourage stockroom personnel to write down any and all errors they uncover, as well as their suggested solutions. Allow time each working day for a brief meeting to discuss all items on the flip chart. This approach allows stockroom personnel to find and resolve most of the problems themselves.

Transaction History File

Regardless of the cycle counting method in use, the most valuable tool for cycle counters is the transaction history file or report (see Figure 5-14, page 86). This report lists, in chronological order, all of the transactions for a specific part, over a specific period of time.

Each transaction can provide clues to the causes of discrepancies. If a part was known to be accurate six weeks ago, and is not today, a review of its transaction history report will exhibit all of the transactions that have taken place for that part over the last six weeks. One or more of these historical transactions will provide valuable clues to the causes of the discrepancy. Effective cycle counting focuses very diligently on finding and fixing the *causes* of errors, not just the errors themselves.

WHO IS RESPONSIBLE FOR CYCLE COUNTING?

Cycle counting is a quality measurement process that belongs in the stockroom, and direct responsibility should be with the stockroom

---

[10] Some firms might want to segment their part number problems by *most costly* errors instead of most frequent.

supervisor. It is in the stockroom, after all, that receiving, storing, and issuing transactions take place. And the counters themselves should be stockroom personnel.

Full-time cycle counters recommended. Some firms assign the cycle counting task to regular stockroom attendants, who include counting among their many daily responsibilities. At other firms, cycle counting is a full-time position. Where staffing capabilities permit, the use of full-time cycle counters is recommended. Typically, companies that utilize part-time counters never provide sufficient time for seeking the causes of errors; this important job is either ignored or handed off to someone else, usually with unsatisfactory results.

Linking responsibility with authority. We should never hold an individual accountable for results unless that person is given the authority to get the job done. A corollary of this principle is that we cannot allow others to meddle in another person's area of responsibility. Thus, if the stockroom supervisor is accountable for maintaining inventory record accuracy, only persons working for or authorized by that supervisor should be able to adjust on-hand balances. In a sense, this principle is analogous to the "limited access" principle cited earlier.

In some firms, material planners have the ability to make unilateral adjustments to on-hand balances. The accountability of the stockroom supervisor cannot be maintained in these situations. It is as if our next-door neighbor was authorized to write checks on our checking account, and at the same time we were held responsible for the account balance. It does not work.

Documenting procedures. Not only must responsibilities be clearly assigned but documentation of cycle counting procedures is also necessary. Like all operational functions, cycle counting needs to be audited occasionally to determine its effectiveness. The technique(s) used for sampling and counting, the procedures followed, and the assignment of responsibility all need to be documented for this auditing purpose.

THE COMPLETION OF THE THREE-PHASE APPROACH

Cycle counting is the final phase in our three-phase approach to establishing and maintaining inventory record accuracy of 95 percent or better. Unlike the first two, it is ongoing. Its methods of error detection act like a compass, indicating when and by how much record accuracy is straying off course. The methods discussed above for determining the root causes of those errors help bring us back on course.

Chapter 8

Inventory Record Accuracy in the Environment of Continuous Improvement

With global competitors dominating many of what were once domestic markets, the Continuous Improvement philosophy of manufacturing is rapidly becoming one of the primary tools of survival for many industrial companies. Firms in many sectors of the manufacturing economy have thrown out the old rule book in favor of new ways of producing goods. Production lines have adapted to shorter runs and faster changeovers. Line workers empowered with multiple skills have been given the opportunity to schedule work, maintain their own equipment, and even stop the production line when quality is in jeopardy. We have begun to see waste in any form—even unnecessary inventory transactions—as the primary enemy.

It is not the authors' purpose to describe Continuous Improvement (CI) and Just-in-Time manufacturing in detail, but rather to recognize their importance and their effects on how inventory records are maintained.[1]

---

[1] For a detailed description of Just-in-Time and Continuous Improvement, see William A. Sandras, Jr., *Just-in-Time: Making It Happen* (Essex Junction, VT: Oliver Wight Limited Publications, Inc., 1989).

INVENTORY ACCURACY AS A QUALITY ISSUE

It is important to realize that CI techniques have virtually no material planning or replanning capabilities. CI techniques are employed to locate and eliminate waste. Therefore, some tool for planning must be used. The most powerful and robust manufacturing planning method in existence today is Manufacturing Resource Planning (MRP II). In fact, the most successful CI applications use one or another type of MRP II for its dependent demand planning ability. Regardless of the form of MRP II, it always uses the fundamental manufacturing equation:

1. What are we going to make?

2. What does it take to make it?

3. What do we have?

4. What do we need to get, and when?

Inventory record accuracy addresses the third question: What do we have? Without the ability to answer this question accurately, it is not possible to answer the fourth question accurately: What do we need to get, and when? A CI application without accurate inventory records quickly reverts to the world of shortage reports and hot lists. The point is simple. Accurate inventory records are a prerequisite for the planning system that supports CI.

Ninety-five percent inventory record accuracy remains the minimum level of accuracy required to maintain a productive MRP II system in any manufacturing environment—traditional or CI. However, this level is challenged by many authorities on Continuous Improvement. Generally, they feel that CI, with its lower inventory levels, requires a higher minimum level of accuracy. All concede that inaccurate inventory records at any level are unacceptable, and they encourage campaigns to drive record accuracy to 100 percent.

One point that all CI authorities agree on, however, is that inventory record accuracy is a quality issue. Therefore, it should be treated as a quality problem and resolved using quality tools. These techniques, as they relate to inventory record accuracy, were briefly described in the preceding cycle counting chapter.

THE CONTINUOUS IMPROVEMENT ENVIRONMENT

Continuous Improvement in manufacturing addresses the elimination of waste within a company at all levels. Waste is defined as anything or any activity that does not add value to the product. Central to the implementation of CI within a manufacturing company is the elimination of inventory, stockrooms, inspection, purchase orders, manufacturing orders, and transactions. Each of these requires a great deal of care and feeding and adds no particular value to the final product.

Some Assumptions

Our purpose here is to describe how inventory record accuracy is maintained in this environment. For this discussion it is assumed that MRP II is being used to plan material. It is also assumed that manufacturing orders or purchase orders have been eliminated and that parts are being stored at the point of use—on the factory floor. While the ideal of CI is to eliminate stockrooms, it is assumed that one stockroom for component parts is still in existence and some parts move through it, while other parts do not. A finished goods stockroom is still used for some finished goods, while other products move directly to the customer upon completion. Inventories have been reduced through the process of Continuous Improvement and are now being turned 20 or more times per year. Kanban signals (defined later) are the predominant material movement authorizations.

WORK-IN-PROCESS VERSUS STOCK (ON-HAND BALANCES)

In a traditional MRP II environment, inventory exists in either one of two formats: work-in-process or stock (on hand). Work-in-process inventory is related to manufacturing orders when a manufacturing order (MO) is released for a parent. The MO references the bill of material for the parent and allocates (reserves) from the component inventory. These allocations are attached to the MO and are specific to it. That is, once they are created for a manufacturing order, they remain attached to it unless manually changed or until the MO is closed. These allocations are listed on the pick list for each particular MO. When component parts are picked from stock and issued to the MO, the components fill, or satisfy, the allocations. The components thus become attached to the work order via the allocations. Manufacturing orders and the issued components represent work-in-process.

When manufacturing orders are not used, as is typically the case in a Continuous Improvement environment, there is technically no WIP with respect to MRP II. All inventory is considered stock. Period. Inventory can be, and usually is, physically located in stockrooms and on the factory floor, and appears on the stock status record as on-hand inventory. When a parent part is manufactured in a Continuous Improvement environment, it does not pass through the work-in-process step with respect to MRP II, as traditionally expected. Rather, the components remain in stock until the parent is manufactured. Upon completion, the parent immediately goes into stock, and the components are automatically deducted from the on-hand inventory.

This approach assumes one or more transactions when another is reported. This greatly reduces the number of transactions traditionally used in authorizing and tracking the manufacture of product. That is, when the parent part is received into stock (one transaction), it is assumed that it was authorized to be built (traditionally another transaction), that all the components necessary were picked and used (traditionally, at least one transaction for each component), the parent was completed (traditionally, another transaction), and the manufacturing order was closed (still another transaction). In the CI environment described above, all of these transactions are assumed upon the receipt transaction of the parent. The benefits of eliminating these other transactions are tremendous in companies that assemble products consisting of many components.

Continuous Improvement pushes us to increase the velocity of products through all phases of their development, production, and distribution. Activities that do not add value are not desirable and are typically the ones that reduce or misdirect this velocity. Transactions are non-value-added activities because they are for internal purposes only, and in many companies, the time required to record them exceeds the actual build time of the product.

THE INVENTORYING PROCESS IN A CONTINUOUS IMPROVEMENT ENVIRONMENT

The best way to understand how the inventorying process works in a Continuous Improvement environment is to follow the flow of material in the example we assumed.

First, visualize parts arriving in the stockroom from a supplier. Most likely, they will be received using a receiving transaction. This puts them on hand, recordwise, in the stockroom. These parts will reside in the stockroom until they are issued. Since manufacturing orders are not used, the impetus to issue the parts must come in the form of a kanban[2] rather than a manufacturing order pick list. When a kanban is the signal for material movement, stock will wait in the stockroom until a kanban card requesting parts arrives from the factory floor. This card specifies the part number, the quantity requested, and the location to which the parts should be sent.

When the parts are picked from the stockroom, a transaction needs to be recorded to tell the inventory records that these parts are now located in a specific workstation location and are no longer in the stockroom. This is a stock-to-stock transfer transaction.

---

[2] Kanban is the driving methodology of Continuous Improvement on the factory floor. Loosely translated, kanban means "card" or "signal." Kanbans may be squares taped or painted on a workbench or the floor, pigeonholes, golf balls, lights, cards, or containers. Whatever their form, says William A. Sandras, Jr., "kanbans are the authorization to do your thing." Your thing may be to perform a manufacturing operation on a part, to move it, ship it, inspect it, or rework it. Kanban is the glue between all customer and supplier relations. When a kanban has been triggered by a customer (downstream) operation, the supplier (upstream) is then authorized to perform whatever that kanban represents. Kanbans on the factory floor to replenish inventory to the floor stocking location work just like a reorder point; that is, when the stock in the factory location goes below a certain level, a kanban card or container is sent to the stockroom for replenishment.

Production of the parent part is authorized in the factory, by either a schedule or a kanban. Either method is acceptable and does not affect this discussion. Upon completion of the parent, it is reported as received. As described earlier, this increases the on-hand quantity of the parent part and simultaneously reduces the on-hand quantity of the components that should have been used to make the parent. The mechanics of the receipt, with respect to the parent, are quite simple and have just been described. However, the mechanics of reducing the components deserve more discussion. The process is technically referred to as *automatic deduction*.

AUTOMATIC DEDUCTION OF MATERIAL OR COMPONENTS

The most common term used for automatic deduction of material or components is *backflushing*. Backflushing is a method of updating inventory records at some defined point in the manufacturing process, called the *deduct point*. All the parts that are assumed to have been used in that process to that point are then deleted from stock. For example, if a computer keyboard was being assembled, the number of keyboards actually manufactured (the deduct point) would be counted, and from that finished quantity the number of component parts would be determined from the bill of materials and "backflushed." If 100 keyboards were finished at the end of the day, it could be assumed that 100 letters a, b, c, d, and so forth were used. These would be deducted from stock; 100 finished keyboards would be added to on-hand stock.

Backflushing should not require a separate transaction but should result from processing an existing transaction—commonly the receipt transaction of a parent part. When processed, it should automatically issue from stock all components assumed to be used in the manufacture of the parent. This assumption is based on the components contained in the bill of material. That is, if parent part 1234 has a bill of material calling for a quantity of 1 component 1111 and 2 components 2222, the automatic deduction transaction for 10 parents 1234 would backflush or issue 10 components 1111 and 20 components 2222 (see Figure 8-1).

Figure 8-1 Automatic Deduct

Transaction	Part Number	Quantity	Date
Receipt	1234	10	2/10

Components	B/M Quantity	Issued
1111	1	10
2222	2	20

Assumptions of Automatic Deduct

To make automatic deduct work properly and result in accurate inventory records, six basic assumptions must be met:

1. *The bill of material (BOM) must be 100 percent accurate.* This first assumption is necessary because automatic deduction references the BOM when generating the automatic issues it uses to reduce component inventories. If the BOM is not 100 percent correct, the wrong components—or the right ones in the wrong quantities—will be deducted from inventory.

2. *All scrap is properly recorded.* Again, automatic deduction reduces inventory using bills of material. When a component is scrapped, the scrappage is not included in the BOM; thus, it will not be deducted from inventory. Scrap must be reported separately and correctly.

3. *All substitutions are properly documented.* If a substitute or alternate part is used, it must be noted; otherwise, automatic deduction will reduce only the parts listed on the bill of material and not those actually used.

4. *Actual locations are used.* When a company maintains its inventory using piece count by multiple locations, it must deduct the components

from their proper locations.[3] If the parts are not deducted from the actual locations, cycle counting is extremely difficult.

5. *Production is correctly reported.* The fifth assumption is that production reporting on the parent part is done correctly. If an incorrect parent is reported, automatic deduction will reduce the on-hand balances of its components and not those of the parent actually made. This, of course, can affect many component part inventory records. Incorrect quantities reported of the parent are multiplied incorrectly through the bills of material to the components. Both situations also adversely affect the on-hand balances of the parent parts.

6. *There is no major delay between the usage of the components and production reporting.* Since component inventories are updated via the automatic deductions triggered by the receipt of the parent, any delay in reporting that receipt will result in an equal delay in component record updating. In a product that contains many pieces, the result of a major delay (greater than one day) can render cycle counting of the component virtually impossible. (Note: When manufacturing processes are lengthy, special deduct or control points can be introduced to prevent major delays between the usage of components and production reporting. See below.)

Deduct Points

In some environments, it becomes essential to have *deduct points* (for automatic-deduct) along an assembly line or its feeder lines. This becomes very important when a product has many pieces and the manufacturing process is lengthy. In these cases, particular points in the process need to be established where a parent subassembly can be reported complete in order to downgrade the components upstream and put the parent into inventory downstream where it was built. Even

---

[3] This process is tricky if a part is a component of multiple parents stored in multiple assembly line locations. This is best accomplished by specifying the deduct location for the part on the part-parent linkage in the bill of material. Thus, when we report a particular parent built, we deduct the components from the specified location. It is important to note that the deduct location is not on the part record or on the parent record but is on the part-parent link in the bill of material.

though the parent subassembly is on the assembly line, it is still considered on hand. Deduct points along the line make reconciliation of cycle counting easy. (Note: Deduct points are established by structuring a parent part number in the bill of material. This is necessary to issue or downgrade the inventory records of the parts that have been consumed.) Figure 8-2 is a graphic representation of a manufacturing workplace with components being added at various workstations. The rectangles represent "deduct points," points at which receiving transactions are made to backflush components and increase the on-hand count of the parent.

Figure 8-2   Deduct Points

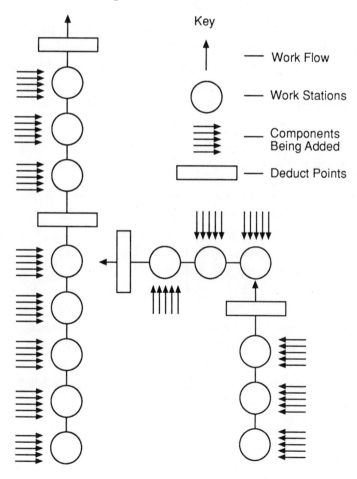

CYCLE COUNTING IN A CI ENVIRONMENT

A major difference in a CI environment is that production workers perform job functions of stock attendants and cycle counters for those parts within their areas. The environment of Continuous Improvement provides many occasions during the day when time is available for those on the line to count parts in their production areas. This might happen when a line is temporarily shut down because of a manufacturing or quality problem, or at the beginning or end of each day. In these cases, operators or assemblers have the opportunity to do cycle counting or periodic inventories.

These counting times occur frequently, and in most instances, the operator or assembler will not be able to count all the parts in each location. However, each person is responsible for maintaining inventory record accuracy for his or her parts. Since there is usually very little inventory in the Continuous Improvement workplace, many part numbers can be counted quickly during these routine line stops.

ADAPTING INVENTORY RECORD ACCURACY TO THE NEW WORKPLACE

The real secret of maintaining accurate inventory records in an environment of Continuous Improvement is understanding the inventorying process and adapting it to high-velocity manufacturing. Techniques such as automatic deducting of inventory have been around for years. Making them work is the real challenge.

Continuous Improvement has introduced more changes in factory floor practices than on the inventorying process and related systems. Eliminating inventory transactions and maintaining inventory record accuracy are directly related to extremely high bills of material accuracy, a proper recording of scrap and substitutions, strict adherence to the kanban rules, low inventory levels, and correct and timely production reporting.

Chapter 9

Accountability

When it comes to managing performance, accountability is key. The same applies to a company's inventory assets—there must be a line of accountability from the very top of the organization to the lowest level at which inventory assets are maintained. Within that line of accountability, however, one person has primary responsibility for accurate inventory records—the stockroom supervisor. For this reason it is important that we understand how to evaluate the performance of the stockroom supervisor with respect to inventory record accuracy.

The best way to start this evaluation is by taking a look at the supervisor's job description. In general terms, the stockroom supervisor's basic functions are planning, organizing, operating, and controlling the varied activities of the warehouse and/or stockroom. The stockroom supervisor may report to the material and capacity planning manager, inventory control manager, distribution manager, or plant manager. He or she is responsible for the hourly labor force of the warehouse and stockroom. If the stockroom operates more than one shift, there may be up to three lead people sharing these responsibilities—one for each shift.

Many firms use formal job descriptions to articulate the specific responsibilities of employees, including stockroom supervisors. These have proven their worth in making the important duties and responsibilities of a position clear to both employees and their managers. Job descriptions can also be used to establish priorities (weights) among the various duties. Most human resources experts recommend that job descriptions be used both to evaluate employee performance and as a means of communication between manager and subordinate.

Figure 9-1 is a hypothetical employee evaluation form. It contains a job description for a stockroom supervisor.[1] It clearly states the basic functions of the position, the reporting relationship, and the supervisory role. Further, it spells out—and often quantifies—particular responsibilities of the job by assigning "weights" to those responsibilities, making it clear which are most important.

In companies that use periodic employee performance reviews, managers sit down with employees and discuss performance with respect to each of the listed job responsibilities. This procedure puts all job-related issues on the table, lets employees know exactly where they stand in terms of the boss's perception of their performance, and gives them an opportunity to discuss issues that impede smooth operations in the workplace.

RESPONSIBILITIES OF STOCKROOM SUPERVISORS

The most important responsibility of the stockroom supervisor, and one that should make up about 70 percent of a performance evaluation, is maintaining accurate inventory record balances. This includes all materials within the stockroom and pertains to that inventory's identification, location, and quantity. This also includes responsibility for maintaining the cycle counting program, even though the cycle counters are ultimately responsible for taking the counts. Nonetheless, the cycle counters report to the stockroom supervisor because they are the stockroom supervisor's primary tool for controlling and monitoring accurate inventory records.

A performance rating for the supervisor should be based on the following accuracy levels:

- *Inadequate*—for inventory records that are less than 90 percent accurate

---

[1] Most firms give employees a written job description when they are hired for a position.

Figure 9-1   Employee Evaluation

NAME		JOB TITLE
		WAREHOUSE/ STOCKROOM SUPERVISOR

DEPARTMENT	RESP. CODE	DATE ASSIGNED TO PRESENT POSITION
MATERIAL & CAPACITY PLANNING		

LOCATION NAME	LOC. CODE	DATE OF LAST EVALUATION

PREPARED BY: JOB DESCRIPTION   DATED

Rating						
Inadequate	Marginal	Satisfactory	Good	Superior		

Basic Function:

Responsible for planning, organizing, operating, and controlling the activities of the warehouse and stockroom areas.

Reports to: Material & Capacity Planning Manager

Supervises: Warehouse and stockroom hourly labor force on a three shift basis (to include up to three lead people).

Responsibilities:

Weight 70%
1. Responsible for maintaining accurate inventory balances with respect to identification, location, and quantity of all production materials within the warehouse and storage areas. Performance rating is based on the following accuracy levels:

   Satisfactory: Inventory is 95% accurate

   Good: Inventory is 96% accurate

   Superior: Inventory is 97%+ accurate

Weight 5%
2. Responsible for receiving all production materials withing 4 hours of arrival on the receiving dock.

Weight 5%
3. Responsible for supporting production with timely and orderly production pulls as scheduled and specified by production control.

Weight 5%
4. Responsible for keeping the warehouse & stockroom neat, orderly, and clean inside and out and minimize hazards to operating safety.

Weight 5%
5. Prepare and administer the warehouse & stockroom operating budget per published procedures and schedules.

Weight 10%
6. Ensure that the warehouse and storage areas operate in "harmony" with the other departments, the adjacent community, and outside suppliers. The supervisor should portray a professional image to each of these entities.

- *Marginal*—for inventory records that are 90 percent to 95 percent accurate

- *Satisfactory*—for inventory records that are 95 percent to 96 percent accurate

- *Good*—for inventory records that are 96 percent to 97 percent accurate

- *Superior*—for inventory records greater than 97 percent accurate

Ninety-five percent accuracy might seem high for "satisfactory" performance, given the low state of accuracy in American industry as a whole, but for the company that uses MRP II or Continuous Improvement manufacturing, 95 percent accuracy is a minimum level of acceptable performance.

The supervisor, however, is responsible for more than maintaining accurate records. Five percent of the supervisor's evaluation should be based on the receiving function; good practice calls for receiving all production materials within four hours of their arrival.

Another 5 percent should be based on the service function. The stockroom is not, after all, a profit center; its job is to support production (its "customer") with the timely and accurate issuing of needed materials. The stockroom supervisor is responsible for support of production with timely and orderly issuing of materials as scheduled and as specified by production control.

Keeping the warehouse and stockroom neat, orderly, and clean inside and out, as well as minimizing hazards to operating safety, is another important responsibility. This, too, should make up 5 percent of the evaluation. Still another 5 percent is based on the preparation and administration of the warehouse and stockroom operating budget per published policies and procedures.

The final 10 percent of the stockroom supervisor's evaluation, and the last of the responsibilities, should consider the degree to which the warehouse and storage areas operate in harmony with the other departments, the adjacent community, and outside suppliers. The supervisor should portray a professional image to each of these entities.

MANAGEMENT REVIEWS

"If it's not broken, don't fix it" is a popular American expression. However, with a "process" like inventory record accuracy that takes months to bring into balance, managers should not wait for evidence that it is broken before they give it their attention. Like driving a car down the highway, it is better to check and adjust the steering periodically than to wait until you are in a ditch.

Cycle counts provide a means to check the inventory on a periodic and continuing basis. One frequently asked question is: How often should management review cycle counting results? These are the recommended forms of review:

1. Management should review the cycle counting numbers weekly *at a minimum* to spot any emerging trends.

2. Cycle count for the past few months. A weekly report should show all the cycle counting that has taken place over the past few months. This report puts the weekly counts into better perspective.

There are primarily three cycle counting reports that offer management a clear view into the stockroom. The first report details what the cycle counting was for the day. The problem with this report is that it reflects only the sample that was counted on that particular day; the numbers provided may not be stable, and because they are based on a small sample, they might not be very representative of the population of inventory records as a whole. If the accuracy level of the daily count is 93 percent, it may mean one of three things: (1) overall inventory accuracy has fallen off abruptly, (2) the counters ran into some problem areas that day, or (3) some combination of 1 and 2. A one-day count can alert us to potential problems but cannot be used to draw firm inferences about the entire inventory record system.

If process control cycle counting is being used, and if the counting is location driven, then a daily report is a reflection of moving from one location to another. To smooth out the fluctuations that characterized daily counts, companies average their cycle counts over some length of time. One approach would be to take today's cycle counting results and average them with all previous daily counts. This would then give an average based on many days' counts. Just how many days should be used to make up the average is a matter of judgment. Using one or two days' counts, as has been explained, might be too low to correctly infer the accuracy of the entire population of records. Using too many days in the average has its own problems, as the following example demonstrates.

A company has been counting for 1,000 days; its average IRA over that long period is 97 percent. Monday's count indicating 85 percent accuracy is added in this pool of counts, but the average accuracy is not deflected by any perceptible amount. Monday's count is just a small drop in a very big bucket. Tuesday's count is a disappointing 82 percent; Wednesday's and Thursday's counts are even worse at 79 percent and 75 percent. The Friday count is a sickening 63 percent.

The counters know that something is amiss, but the managers—who receive a weekly report of the long-term average accuracy—have no reason for concern. As far as they know, average inventory record accuracy is still about 97 percent.

Using an "average" based on many daily counts clearly eliminates the "noise" that each day's count creates. But in the case above, the average of 97 percent is so *heavily weighted* toward past counts that it tells management little or nothing about the accuracy of their inventory today. And for operational purposes, today's inventory situation is more important than what it was two years ago.[2] Current trends are simply absorbed in the mass of historical data.

What is needed is a method of reporting that neither whipsaws with daily fluctuations nor masks current trends under the weight of past figures. The best method for reporting for operational effectiveness is to use one or several *moving averages.*

A moving average is simply the average of some defined period that is continually moved forward. Thus, a "two-week moving average" is made of counts from the latest two-week period. Using the weeks in the year as an example, as we enter week 23, weeks 21 and 22 would make up our two-week moving average. Once the counts for week 23 have

---

[2] The longer the period covered in the average, the more it is biased toward past data.

been completed, week 21 drops out and weeks 22 and 23 make up the new moving average.

This method serves the dual purpose of filtering out the fluctuations of daily counts, and focusing attention on the current state of inventory accuracy—not what happened in the distant past. The recommended method of reporting daily cycle counting is to provide several moving averages—each capturing a different-size time frame—as follows:

Process Control Record Accuracy

Last Week	96.2 percent
Last Four Weeks	97.4 percent
Last Eight Weeks	97.3 percent

This process takes the percentage from the first cycle counting day and averages it with counts from the second, third, fourth, and fifth days. This then becomes the Last Week average reflected above. The Last Four Weeks and the Last Eight Weeks are the moving averages of the past four and eight weekly counts respectively.

Companies should report their accuracy in a weekly report to key functional managers. This written report might also contain a graph of weekly averages for the past six months. Reporting in this manner makes trends easy to spot. Other personnel should get the same numbers. Managers are not the only ones who benefit from this important information. Non-managerial personnel benefit from knowing how well (or how poorly) inventory record accuracy is being maintained. The philosophy of Continuous Improvement that so many manufacturing firms are trying to adopt supports this notion fully. Accuracy reports should be posted on a large sign and highly visible in the stockroom and other appropriate locations, much as a bank posts its current interest rates.

ELIMINATING THE PHYSICAL INVENTORY

Over and above the benefits of gaining control of its physical assets, maintaining an inventory record accuracy ≥95 percent allows a company to do away with the physical inventory. As we have mentioned throughout this book, it's important to recognize that physical inventories are not a good practice, and firms should eliminate them as they adopt the processes described in this book. But there is an accountability aspect to the elimination of physical inventories that needs to be addressed here since that procedure has traditionally been the basis for verifying inventory figures that translate into financial values of interest to shareholders, creditors, and other outside parties.

The question is: How do we eliminate the practice of taking physical inventories? Many companies go through a great deal of unnecessary worry and concern over this issue, often because of a misguided notion that they are obliged by the requirements of their auditors to take physical inventories. Outside auditors, however, do not require companies to perform a physical inventory. Their job is to review company policies and procedures to make sure that they make good business and legal sense. They also check to see if those policies and procedures are being followed. If a company's policy states that it will take a physical inventory every year to quantify the assets called inventory, then the auditors are going to make sure that the company takes a physical inventory. This is why the first step in eliminating physical inventories is often for top management to change company policy. A clear policy statement that physical inventories will be eliminated in favor of a program of cycle counting is what is needed.

A cycle counting program to verify the accuracy of inventory records is an acceptable substitute for the traditional physical inventory. Every one of the major national CPA firms has clients who *do not* take physical inventories. These companies can dollarize their inventory records and present them to outside auditors as an accurate statement of their inventory assets. If a company establishes "no physical inventories" as a written policy, that is exactly what the CPAs will audit. The auditors want to know, "Does the policy make sense?" If the answer is "yes," they will ask, "Do the procedures support the policy? Are there procedures in place that tell people how to accurately track and report inventory movement? Are there effective procedures in place that tell people how to perform cycle counting?" If the answer to all of these questions is "yes," the auditors will verify that the company is following those procedures and that they are getting the desired results—accurate inventory records.

Chapter 10

Looking Back and Looking Forward

The challenge of attaining and maintaining an inventory record accuracy of 95 percent and higher has now been laid out. Whether your company is running its operations with a formal system or not, knowing what you have and where it's located is imperative for making what you want. If you are unable to maintain a checkbook account of your assets, you will never really know when a check may bounce, shutting down operations and possibly costing you twice as much to cover your error.

LOOKING BACK

This book has explained the necessity for accurate records and has presented an achievable goal—a minimum of 95 percent accuracy and the elimination of the physical inventory.

Earlier chapters have provided a three-phase approach to achieving that goal: design of the inventorying process, establishing initial balances, and maintaining inventory accuracy through cycle counting.

LOOKING FORWARD

There is a story circulating through the manufacturing world about the "Factory of the Future." This thoroughly modern and scientifically designed facility contains hundreds of robotic machines, a dog, and a man. In this factory, the machines do all the work. The man is there to feed the dog. And the dog is there to make sure that the man does not touch the machines.

Futurists and other dreamers are happy to think that this is how manufacturing will be done someday. The problem with this vision is, in our view, the subservient role of (wo)man. First, it assumes that people would rather live in a world in which they have little to do that resembles work. There are at least two of us around who would dispute that assumption. Many people still identify with and are fulfilled by work. Second, the passive role of man in this story is at odds with the most dynamic examples of manufacturing that we can find today.

The best manufacturing facilities today are characterized by a high level of interaction between all personnel and the production process. There is no dog to keep people from touching the machines, from rearranging and adjusting them, or from poking around for a way to make things work better. These are facilities where people are actively looking for ways to improve not just the product but the hundreds of processes that make the product. Take care of the process, they have learned, and the rest will follow. This is what Continuous Improvement is all about.

The process we have just described for establishing and maintaining inventory record accuracy is one of those many processes. Like the others, it needs to be touched, rearranged, and adjusted by people on a regular basis because we always assume that it can be improved.

So from an inventorying process perspective, what might the "Factory of the Future" look like? Consider Figure 10-1. This factory is enclosed within the heavy rectangle, and everything inside that rectangle is in stock. There is no stockroom here, no inspection point, no finished goods storeroom, no overload area. Certainly there is very little transactional tracking as parts move from Work Station A to Work Station D using kanban signals, and inventory balances are maintained using the automatic deduction techniques described in Chapter 8.

This futuristic factory seems elegant in its simplicity. Indeed, it does not require any robotics, and dogs would only be in the way. But it does require people to find ways to make it work better. The inventory

Figure 10-1 Factory of the Future

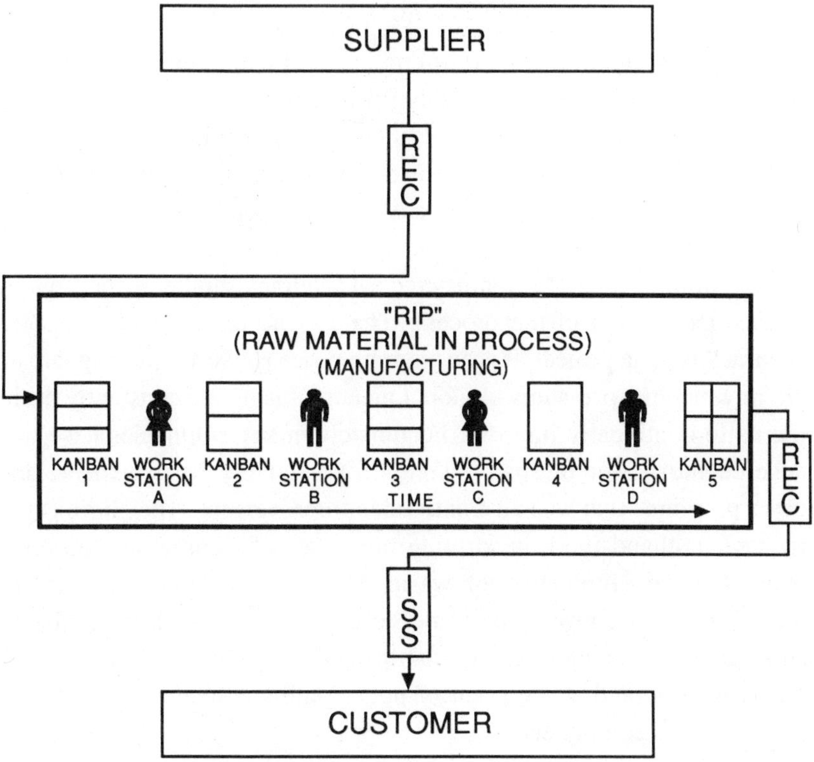

Criteria:

- Short Lead Times
- Short Cycle Times (Small Queues)
- Little or No Safety Stock
- Quality at Source
- Daily Deliveries
- No Lot Sizing
- Kanban or Demand Pull in Place

system, too, would have to be elegantly simple—literally transparent. But the need for it would never go away entirely.

Inventory record accuracy is a continual pursuit, which is why the ongoing phase of cycle counting explained in this book is so imperative. Once management is able to see the consistency developed by these techniques, the decision can be made to dismantle the physical inventory process. That decision is, in a way, a first step toward the futuristic vision sketched here.

The ultimate goal of inventory record accuracy should be the Continuous Improvement of the process. There is no end. Inventory record accuracy is not a project, it is an ongoing process. We are moving into an era in which the pressures of global manufacturing are constantly pushing us to continually improve. Fortunately, many companies have discovered the power of Just-in-Time, Total Quality Management, and other programs that we call Continuous Improvement. They have experienced firsthand the transforming processes of Continuous Improvement and the elimination of waste. However, without an inventory record accuracy above 95 percent, these companies would be unable to address the elimination of manufacturing orders, the accurate accounting of parts stored at the point of use, or the automatic deductions of materials and components.

Glossary

ABC Classification Classification of inventory parts in descending order of annual dollar volume or some other criterion. This array is subdivided into classes, A, B, C. Class A parts are those with the highest dollar volume (or other criterion) and receive the closest attention. Class C contains the lowest dollar volume items. The classification method is used to focus limited attention on highest priority parts.

ABC cycle counting A cycle counting technique that is explicitly biased toward parts that represent a greater inventory investment. The ABC cycle counting process puts an explicit bias on the samples to reflect the monies invested in inventory. Simply explained, the "A" class parts (the 20 percent of the parts that represents 80 percent of the total monies spent per year on inventory) are counted more frequently than the "B" and "C" class parts, which account for lesser expenditures.

Accuracy Within acceptable limits from a given standard.

Allocation Allocations are reservations for parts that have not yet been withdrawn or issued from stock. An allocated part is thus "reserved" and not available for other purposes.

Available inventory On-hand inventory less allocated inventory.

Backflushing The deduction from inventory of the component parts used in a parent by exploding the bill of materials by the production cost of parents produced.

Bill of Material A listing of components, parts, and other items needed to manufacture a product, showing the quantity of each required. A bill of material is similar to a parts list except that it usually shows how the product is fabricated and assembled. Also called a formula, recipe, or ingredients list.

Component/parent part A part, ingredient, or subassembly that is both a component to a higher level part, and a parent part to other components.

Component part Raw material, ingredient, part, or subassembly that goes into a higher level assembly, compound, or other part.

Continuous Improvement (CI) A term that describes the many management practices and techniques used to find and eliminate waste. A more descriptive term for the practices of Just-in-Time manufacturing.

Control group cycle counting Counting the same parts in the same locations repeatedly within a very short time frame. If the design of the inventory process has flaws, they should be observable in the control group of parts. The parts counted are the "control group." Control group cycle counting is used for verifying the new design of the inventory process. It is the only form of cycle counting not truly used to measure inventory record accuracy.

Cycle counting Regular daily counts of on-hand parts. A method of maintaining inventory record accuracy by the systematic counting of parts and the finding of discrepancies between records and actual counts and the sources of those discrepancies. A number of different approaches to selecting parts to be counted, and the frequency of those counts, are used.

Deduct point The point in the production process up to which all the parts assumed to have use (as defined in the bill of material) are "backflushed," (automatically deducted) from the inventory records. Also see Backflushing.

Finished goods Inventory to which the final increments of value have been added through manufacturing.

Inventorying process Includes the receiving of parts, putting them away, and their storage, withdrawal, issue, and movement through work-in-process, while simultaneously tracking their movement and maintaining records of those events and their effects.

Inventory records Hard copy or electronic documents that reflect how much and what kind of inventories a company has on hand, committed (allocated) to work in process, and on order.

Issue list A document that states all the parts to be issued.

Issue tickets Specially coded authorizations to withdraw allocated stock items from the stockroom. When presented to the stockroom, they can be exchanged for the parts designated.

Issuing documents The physical documents that communicate specifically how much of what needs to be issued to where. Issue lists, issue tickets, and issue decks are all forms of issuing documents.

Just-in-Time (JIT) A manufacturing management approach that focuses on the ongoing and relentless pursuit of the elimination of waste. JIT encompasses an ever-growing set of practices and techniques to find and eliminate waste. More and more practitioners are using the term "Continuous Improvement" (CI) to describe these practices and techniques (see Continuous Improvement).

Kanban A Just-in-Time/Continuous Improvement production method in which consuming (downstream) operations pull from feeding (upstream) operations. Feeding operations are authorized to produce only after receiving a kanban card (or "signal") from the consuming operation.

Manufacturing order An order to the manufacturing facility authorizing the production of parent parts or component/parent parts.

Manufacturing Resource Planning (MRP II) A method for the effective planning of the physical, human, and financial resources of a manufacturer. It addresses operational planning in units and financial planning in dollars, and has a simulation capacity. Sometimes described as a management system based on network scheduling.

Material Requirements Planning (MRP) An approach to calculating material requirements not only to generate replenishment orders but also to reschedule open orders to meet changing requirements. Once viewed strictly as an inventory ordering technique, MRP is thought of today as more of a scheduling technique.

Materials management The organizational grouping of the functions related to the complete cycle of material flow, from purchasing to the planning and control of work-in-process, to warehousing, shipping, and distribution of finished goods.

Moving average The average of some defined period that is continually moved forward. Thus, a "two-week moving average" is made of counts from the latest two-week period. A moving average biases the average of historical information to the more recent periods.

MRP See Material Requirement Planning.

MRP II See Manufacturing Resources Planning.

On-hand balance Quantity of an item shown in the inventory records as being physically in stock.

Order point inventory system A system in which a specified record quantity signals a reorder of an existing stock item; that is, a reorder notice is generated and sent to a supplier when the on-hand inventory balance reaches a specified level.

Parent part Any finished goods, end item, or part that is mixed, fabricated, assembled, stirred, or blended from one or more other components.

Pareto Principle A heuristic rule which states that where there is a large number of contributors to a result, the majority of the result is due to a minority of the contributors (the 80/20 rule). The basis of ABC analysis.

Percentage inventory records accuracy The sum of the accurate records divided by the sum of the records checked (both accurate and inaccurate).

Physical inventory The actual counting of items on hand with the objective of recalibrating inventory records.

Picking Collecting items from a storage location to satisfy a shop or customer order.

Picking list A form or document used by stockroom attendants to pick stockroom items. The list indicates both the items or part numbers and their respective quantities.

Process control cycle counting A highly productive type of cycle counting that is biased toward counting parts with low on-hand balances and those with obvious errors. Refer to Chapter 7 for more information.

Purchase order An order to a vendor authorizing the delivery of materials.

Random sample cycle counting A method in which the particular parts to be counted are selected from the population of part numbers in a manner that has no inherent bias. In this selection process, each part number has an equal chance of being selected.

Sample stability If a sample produces a particular result and by increasing the sample size it continues to produce the same result, the sample has *stability* and can be assumed to be a reliable representation of the population. This is an important characteristic when the population size is unknown or extremely large.

Systematic physical inventory A hybrid of traditional physical inventory and cycle counting methods. The recommended approach to calibrating initial balances. Refer to Chapter 6 for additional information.

Transaction Recording of a material movement or adjustment event.

Work-in-process (WIP) Product in any of various stages of the value adding within the plant.

Index